EVERY DAY IS
GAME DAY

EVERY DAY IS GAME DAY

Fran Tarkenton
with Jim Bruton

TRIUMPH
BOOKS

Library of Congress Cataloging-in-Publication Data

Tarkenton, Fran.
  Every day is game day / Fran Tarkenton with Jim Bruton.
    p. cm.
  ISBN 978-1-60078-253-4
  1. Tarkenton, Fran. 2. Football players—United States—Biography.
3. Quarterbacks (Football)—United States—Biography. I. Bruton, Jim. II. Title.
  GV939.T3E93 2009
  796.332092—dc22
  [B]
                                                        2009017452

This book is available in quantity at special discounts for your group or organization. For further information, contact:
    Triumph Books
    542 South Dearborn Street
    Suite 750
    Chicago, Illinois 60605
    (312) 939-3330
    Fax (312) 663-3557
    www.triumphbooks.com

Printed in U.S.A.
ISBN: 978-1-60078-253-4
Design by Patricia Frey

Photo credits: pages 11, 161, 173, and 183 courtesy of the Tarkenton family; pages v, 1, 49, 57, 65, 79, 91, 107, 135, and 147 courtesy of the Minnesota Vikings; pages 27 and 41 courtesy of AP Images; and page 123 courtesy of Getty Images.

Contents

Foreword

Having played the quarterback position in the National Football League for 11 years, I can attest to the fact that Fran Tarkenton was one of the greatest players of all time. His record performance in 18 NFL seasons with the Minnesota Vikings and the New York Giants cemented his induction into the Pro Football Hall of Fame. Nine Pro Bowls, a Pro Bowl Most Valuable Player Award, the College Football Hall of Fame, and numerous other accolades solidify Fran's accomplishments among the best who ever played the game.

Fran was as difficult to defend as any quarterback we ever played against. He drove defensive coaches absolutely crazy as they tried to put together game plans to control and contain him. He could literally do anything—throw deep down the field; make first downs with short, high-percentage passes; or destroy you with scrambling bursts that were virtually unstoppable.

We played many great games against each other and always enjoyed being together, whether in competitive action on the field, as teammates at the Pro Bowl, or off the field.

This book is a fascinating story that takes the reader through Fran's entire life, from the alleys of Washington, D.C. to the streets of Athens, Georgia. We follow his great career through high school, at the University of Georgia, and professionally with the Minnesota

Vikings and the New York Giants. The book is filled with anecdotes of past games and great players, including an entire chapter on our famous 1975 playoff game, in which the Hail Mary pass was born.

Fran's fame on the field is consistent with his success as an entrepreneur, as you will discover. Fran is my hero and it has been an honor for me to play against him for so many years and to be great friends. He is one of a kind.

His book will entertain you, make you laugh, and for the first time ever allow you into the world of Fran Tarkenton that few people know. He shares countless personal stories and anecdotes. It is a never-before-told personal journey through his life. I'm glad that I had the opportunity to join him.

—Roger Staubach

Introduction

There was never a dull moment! A November day was usually bone-chilling, with a swirling wind that made playing conditions all but intolerable. The snow was piled up at both ends of the field. The playing surface was harder than concrete. The green-painted dirt on the field bore only a slight resemblance to grass. Fans froze in their seats; being on the summit of Mount Everest in blizzard conditions might have been a welcome alternative.

It was, simply put, cold and miserable. But that's the way it was in late fall at the old Metropolitan Stadium in Bloomington, Minnesota, and even at Yankee Stadium in New York. It was where the Men of Purple roamed and Football Giants played on Sunday afternoons. It was professional football, the very best in entertainment. It was the National Football League and for 18 glorious seasons, he was the leader.

Fans in Minnesota and New York acclimated to the severe conditions as the seasons passed because once the game got under way, it rarely mattered. What transpired on those special Sundays heated up their chilled bodies and warmed their hearts. And for almost two decades they watched and cheered No. 10—and there was never a dull moment, never a boring minute, never a monotonous second.

He made fans rise from their seats and stand in absolute astonishment as he streaked across the tundra from one side to the other. He gave chase, and when it appeared that he was caught, he would break free, and the chase would start all over again.

Mick Tingelhoff, center for the Minnesota Vikings for 17 years, remembers, "I never worried if I missed my block, I would just wait a while and my man would be back."

He ran and they followed. He was smaller than the rest and would likely crumble if his pursuers caught him at once. But they rarely ever did. Instead, he ran, he threw, and he won.

He was a Viking and a Giant. He was often victorious on the field, but he was always victorious in the hearts of the fans. He was their leader, their conquering hero, and he never surrendered.

His name is Francis Asbury Tarkenton, and he remains one of the most beloved quarterbacks in the history of football. For 13 years with the Vikings and five with the Giants, his fans watched him in amazement. Some called him "the Scrambler" because he moved so skillfully and gracefully around the field. He brought long-lasting excitement to the fans in the stands, the television viewers, and his teammates.

Whether he was playing high school or college football in Georgia or leading the Vikings or the New York Giants, he was a leader and an inspiration. He wanted to win and gave everything of himself to make it happen. He was something special to everyone who watched him.

Every Day Is Game Day is the first autobiography by one of the greatest gladiators of the gridiron, Fran Tarkenton, with never-before-told stories of his career and life. From his football beginnings in Washington, D.C.; Athens High School; and the University of Georgia; Tarkenton takes you inside the huddle of the big games and on the field for his famous plays, including the 1975 playoff game with the Dallas Cowboys and the one play that still haunts him.

He reflects on his love for Bud Grant, Jerry Burns, Allie Sherman, and Alex Webster; Georgia Bulldogs football; his family and friends in life; the players he admires and respects; and life after the National Football League, from *Monday Night Football* to *That's Incredible!*

The practices, uniforms, and the swelling stadium crowds are decades removed from his routine, but for Fran Tarkenton the game goes on. And he plays it every day with the same grit, dedication, and love in his business and personal life.

This is not a book about football or a book about a football player. This is a book about a remarkable human being—his life, memories, accomplishments, beliefs, and disappointments. Here, in these pages, is the story of the man behind the No. 10, for whom *every day is game day*.

—Jim Bruton

CHAPTER 1

Hail Mary

And the reality is, if we had won the game it likely would have lived in my memories as just another victory among many others. Instead, it was the worst day of my life.

People ask me if, after all these years, I still think about it. The answer is always instantaneous and emphatic: *All the time!*

It was December 28, 1975, and the Dallas Cowboys had come to the "Old Met." The Vikings were heavily favored to win the game, coming off a spectacular NFC-best 12–2 season. But it was not to be. Our 17–14 loss knocked us out of the playoffs, ended one of our greatest seasons, and I believe changed the history of the National Football League forever.

It's reasonable to suppose that I am haunted by the infamous Roger Staubach "Hail Mary" completion to Drew Pearson in the game's final seconds. Or by the previous play, when Pearson caught the fourth-and-17 pass, which was ruled a first down even though the receiver should have been called out of bounds.

But the moment of the game that torments me is something else entirely.

Staubach, a friend and a wonderful person, had a marvelous collegiate and National Football League career. He is a Heisman Trophy winner from the Naval Academy and a Pro Football Hall of Famer who led the Cowboys to four Super Bowl appearances and two championships. He was a great NFL quarterback, and certainly in my top three as the best that ever played the game.

Drew Pearson was one of the premier receivers in the game. Named to the NFL's All-Decade Team for the 1970s, he scored 50 touchdowns in his career with Dallas.

If Staubach had finished his career with one less touchdown pass and Pearson had caught one less in his outstanding seasons with the Cowboys, it wouldn't have diminished their legacies, but it would have lifted a powerful regret for me. The play that still bothers me came when the Vikings last had the ball. It was late in the game and we were midfield, with a third down and 3 or 4. With a first down, the game is over, Dallas does not get the ball back, Staubauch doesn't throw the Hail Mary pass, and the Vikings advance to the NFC Championship game, and beyond.

In the fall of 2008, I was watching television at my lake home and happened to turn on the NFL Network. I rarely watch old NFL game replays, but this one immediately caught my attention. It was that fateful playoff game. And for the first time since the events of the game unfolded more than 30 years ago, I watched the entire game.

I had never watched a replay of it, never looked at the game films, and had no intention of ever doing so. I don't know why, but that day I watched the whole game. The emotions of the day were rekindled immediately. I knew the outcome wouldn't be different, yet I watched. The results remained the same, as did the hurt of losing.

The 1975 Minnesota Vikings were our best team. We had great players and superior coaches. We could run the ball, throw the ball, and score points. Our defense was exceptional. We had everything going for us that year and particularly in that Dallas game.

We had finished the regular season 12–2, losing only to the Washington Redskins 31–30 in Week 11, and to the Detroit Lions 17–10 on the second-to-last week of the season. We had won the first 10 games that year including routing the Browns 42–10, winning 28–3 against the Chicago Bears, and defeating our hated rivals, the Green Bay Packers, 28–17 and 24–3. We wrapped up the regular season by beating the Buffalo Bills 35–13 and were extremely confident going into the playoffs against the Cowboys.

I knew we were going to win, and I remained convinced of it until the very end. I still have a hard time accepting the outcome. And the reality is, if we had won the game, it likely would have lived in my memories as just another victory among many others. Instead, it was the worst day of my life.

To add insult to injury, a new term, *Hail Mary*, entered football's lexicon. And in every game that followed, from Pop Warner to the

NFL, a desperation pass thrown toward the end zone at the end of the half or final seconds of the game is a Hail Mary, and a lingering reminder of that fateful December afternoon in 1975.

As the game ventured into the final quarter, we clearly had things under control. We had a 14–10 lead and showed no signs of relinquishing it. Our defense had been terrific all day. Late in the game, we had a third-down-and-short. If we can convert on this play, we run down the clock and win.

> *"I remember every part of the moment. He wanted the responsibility on his shoulders."*
>
> —JERRY BURNS, FORMER OFFENSIVE COORDINATOR AND HEAD COACH, MINNESOTA VIKINGS

Dallas called a timeout; I think their last for the game. I went over to the sideline to talk to Jerry Burns, our offensive coordinator. We needed to come up with a play to keep the ball and control the ending of the game.

Before another word about the moment in one of the most important football games of my life, I would be greatly remiss if I didn't say something about Jerry Burns. I *love* Jerry Burns! He is the funniest man I have ever known and a brilliant, exceptional football coach and offensive coordinator. We worked closely together and made a great team. We always listened to each other and constantly brainstormed our knowledge and passion for the game. He had a keen understanding of the game and I loved planning game strategies with him.

If asked, I can just imagine Jerry saying, "Fran and I got along great. I always gave him everything he wanted." Now, I would differ with Burnsie on that, and to say we worked well together would not do the relationship justice. It was more than that; I truly loved Jerry Burns!

When I came to the sideline during the game to discuss that third-down play, Burnsie felt that a running play was our best chance to keep possession. I was convinced we should try a rollout to the right side and that I could run for the first down, or at the very least have a great opportunity to toss a short pass to Chuck Forman for the necessary yardage. My self-assurance was enough to convince Jerry, and I went back into the game, confident that we had made the right play call, and that the play would work. There is no question that I was in a position to make the right play call, and most importantly make the play work. Jerry Burns always believed in me and he felt that the quarterback had to run the play, and needed to be confident in the play working.

> *"We had a difference of opinion…on that crucial third down, but I always felt that the guy taking the snap from center is the one that has to make the play work."*
>
> —JERRY BURNS

Unfortunately, Dallas had the play read, almost as though they had been a part of the sideline discussion. Dallas defensive back Charlie Waters burst through the line and the play completely collapsed. We had no chance.

And that one decision I made at that precise moment at the most crucial time in the game, that's what haunts me! There is absolutely no doubt in my mind the decision cost us the game, and an eventual Super Bowl victory, with our greatest team. I should have gone with Burnsie's running play. It hurts to relive it. I have never told that story before.

I mentioned early on that I truly believe that game on December 28, 1975, against the Cowboys changed National Football League history. It certainly changed history for the Minnesota Vikings. If we had won, we may well have gone on to win the Super Bowl. And who knows what it would have meant beyond that. I certainly think that greats like Jim Marshall and Mick Tingelhoff would have been enshrined in the Hall of Fame.

We dominated the league in the 1970s. We did it as much as Pittsburgh, the 49ers, or the Miami Dolphins of that era. But I didn't realize then, as I do today, how important it is to win the Super Bowl. We did well, but we never won that last one, so we will never be associated with those great teams of the past.

*   *   *

The ending of the game and unfair turnabout were deeply upsetting for the players, the coaches, and the fans. It really took a toll on all of us. I had been badgered for interviews by the media after the game and refused. It was not time to do television or radio interviews; it was time to leave the stadium and be with my family.

Grady Alderman and Mick Tingelhoff, my closest friends on the team, and our families had gathered in the parking lot after the game. We had planned to celebrate our win by watching the second game of the day's playoff doubleheader on television and tailgating in a van we had rented.

The mood was already somber when legendary announcer Jack Buck reported on the live broadcast, "We would like to express our condolences to the Tarkenton family for the unexpected death of Fran's father, Dallas Tarkenton, who died this afternoon of a heart attack." I was stunned. It was the first I had heard the news. Reported on national television, in the parking lot at Metropolitan Stadium, I learned of my father's death. I found out at the same time as the rest of the country.

My father was my heart and soul. It was as tough for me as anything could possibly have been. He was filling in as pastor at a small church near Savannah, Georgia, and was at home watching the game with my mom and my older brother, Dallas. I had last spoken to him on Christmas Day a few days before. I was told it was sometime around the middle of the game that he suffered a massive heart attack and was rushed to the hospital. We believe he died before reaching the emergency room.

I deeply loved my father. He was such a decent human being and I was so proud of him. He was not an astute follower of the game of football. He had no clue whether a football was blown up or stuffed but he watched the games because I was playing, and he always supported everything I did. He reveled in my success because he was proud of my accomplishments. And I was proud of my own accomplishments on the field, more than anything because it made *him* proud. Nothing was more important to me than that. He meant so much to me.

I have always felt that my father knew how much I loved him, and I never felt that I missed an opportunity to express my feelings and thoughts to him. He will always have a presence with me. He was always there for me and he still is today.

*   *   *

It took a long time to get anyone from the Minnesota Vikings into the Pro Football Hall of Fame. Eventually, I got in, along with Alan Page, Bud Grant, Carl Eller, Paul Krause, and Ron Yary, among others. But what about Jim Marshall and Mick Tingelhoff? Of all my teammates over the years, I believe Jim and Mick belong in the Hall of Fame more than any of the rest of us.

Jim Marshall never missed a game. He was a great player and dynamic leader. He played in 282 consecutive games! Mick was the Vikings center for 17 years. He was All-Pro for seven consecutive seasons. He was the long snapper on punts, field goals, and extra points. Those Super Bowl losses have deprived the Vikings of so much glory and, without a doubt in my mind, they have kept two of the sport's greatest players from entering the Hall of Fame.

I had an amazing career in the National Football League as the quarterback of the Minnesota Vikings, the New York Giants, and the Vikings again. I played with great players and magnificent coaches. I loved everything about the game and what I did for a living. But that day, that game, and the results have left me with lifelong regrets.

For some, it's easy to recall the famous Hail Mary play and the game results; for me, it is agony. I know that many Vikings fans have lived with the memory of this game and the monumental loss for more than 30 years. My friend Dick Howell told me a long time ago that the fans would like to hear from me about it. I think that I have now done that. It's not much consolation, but it haunts me as much as anyone.

The outcome of the game and the disappointment it has caused for the organization, players, coaches, and fans seems unfair. And coupled with the death of my dad that very same day, it remains the most devastating day of my life.

CHAPTER 2

Alleys to Athens

Throwing a forward pass to Dallas on a crossing pattern to the left of the garbage cans past the second garage on the right—it brought a fire to my belly that carried me through almost three decades of football. Every minute of it was special to me, and I wanted to win.

*G*o down to the second garage on the right and cut to the left at the garbage cans. I'll hit you across the middle.

It was alley football, and I played it with my older brother, Dallas, and anyone we could get to play against us. The alleys were narrow; only one car could pass through them at a time. It helped us learn to be quick and how to be accurate with our throws.

It was a long way from Athens High School, the University of Georgia, the Minnesota Vikings, or the New York Giants, but the intensity and the desire to win and be successful was just as strong back then as at any time in my career.

Throwing a forward pass to Dallas on a crossing pattern to the left of the garbage cans past the second garage on the right—it brought a fire to my belly that carried me through almost three decades of football. Every minute of it was special to me, and I wanted to win.

We lived at 4100 5th Street N.W. in Washington, D.C. Narrow alleys stretched behind our neighborhood's houses, and there were garbage cans outside every garage providing further obstruction. I started throwing the football in those alleys with my brother when I was six or seven years old.

Dallas is a couple years older than me and was a wonderful athlete. He was bigger, taller, faster, and smarter than me. He was a phenomenal receiver; I could throw the ball anywhere and he would go up and get it. We beat everyone and I got used to winning.

I was born with an incredible desire and competitive spirit to win. It doesn't matter if it is football, checkers, golf, or anything else—I want to win! And it has always been that way.

I would pretend to be Redskins great Sammy Baugh, and later on, Jack Scarbath, quarterback from the University of Maryland. In fact, Scarbath is the reason that I have always worn No. 10 on my jersey. (It took me 55 years to discover something about that No. 10 that I will reveal later. It is truly an *incredible* story!)

Scarbath was a great quarterback. I loved the way he played the game. He was an All-American, engineered a perfect 10–0 season, was a Heisman Trophy runner-up, and had a record of 24–4–1 as the Terps' signal caller. He was elected to the College Football Hall of Fame in 1983 and played three years in the National Football League. I really admired him.

Sports, from the time I could first breathe, were a part of my life. It was all I thought about; I had no other interests. I collected bubble-gum cards and played in the D.C. alleys, the playgrounds, the yards, and anywhere there was a game to play or a place to practice.

I was born in Richmond, Virginia and my family moved to Washington, D.C., when I was 5 years old. By the time I was 6 years old, I was into neighborhood football, basketball, and baseball. There was always a game somewhere, and I was a part of it.

It didn't take long for me to develop an interest in professional sports. In addition to Scarbath at Maryland, I lived and died with the Washington Redskins and their great quarterback Sammy Baugh, and the Washington Senators baseball team.

Baugh consumed my thoughts as a child, and to this day he remains a hero. Recently, in talking with a friend, I made the decision to visit the legendary NFL giant at his ranch in Texas. I had never met him, but I wanted him to know how important he was to me as a youngster and how I have idolized his on-field greatness throughout my entire life. He was always with me in those alleys as I looked for Dallas to break loose to the left of the garbage cans. Unfortunately, the very day I made the decision to go to Texas was the day that Baugh died at his home. He was 94.

We moved to Athens, Georgia, from Washington, D.C. when I was 10 years old. So there I was, a Yankee in the South. Athens became my home, and was a wonderful place to grow up. My heart and my roots will always remain in the South. For the past many years, I have made Atlanta a home for me and my family. Atlanta is truly a great city, an international city. It has all the major sports teams, the largest airport in the world, and has 5 million people—and it's growing. Every part of the city is unique. My world here in Atlanta centers on my family and my business, and I am proud to say that all my loved ones are within minutes of my work and my home.

But when I first moved to Georgia, I was steadfast about one thing: I wasn't going to change my sports loyalties. So I remained the University of Maryland's biggest fan. And what about Sammy Baugh and the Redskins? Was I going to leave them too? Not a chance! I kept up with Scarbath and Baugh and never lost the faith with my roots.

I was steadfast about one thing: I wasn't going to change my sports loyalties.

Scarbath was a split-T quarterback. I remember when he came down to Georgia and beat them in a huge game. It really solidified my own identity. Later, when a professional football career was on the horizon, I wanted to play for the Washington Redskins. Even though the Redskins and the Washington Senators were consistently losers, it didn't matter—they were my teams. I always thought it was interesting that when I came to the Minnesota Vikings in 1961, my Washington Senators were relocated and became the Minnesota Twins. I couldn't have mapped out the plan better myself!

My dad relocated us to Athens so he could pursue a Ph.D. in religion and education at the University of Georgia. He grew up dirt poor in a tough section of Norfolk, Virginia. His father was a policeman and died when Dad was nine or 10 years old and his mother died when he was 15. He basically raised his younger sister while living with an aunt.

Dad was a little guy, very intense and brilliant. He was tougher than nails and feisty, but a goodhearted and pure human being. He was an incredible entrepreneur and I had the good fortune of learning from him. Dad loved education, and he attended Holmes Bible College in Greenville, South Carolina before attending the University of Georgia.

He was the smartest and best businessman that I ever knew. When we moved to Athens, he made $40 per week with three children to support. He was skilled at buying houses and renting them out to survive. My mom helped by cleaning rooms. As a team, they did just fine.

* * *

In all honesty, it didn't matter to me where we lived. I would have been happy in Nome, Alaska, and I would have found a way to play and enjoy sports. In D.C., I used to go down to the Uline Arena to watch high school basketball games with my brother and my friends. I loved it! I was also a member of the Merrick Boys Club. Tom Penrod was my first coach in organized sports.

I was enamored by the city and everything that went on there. I remember when General MacArthur came to Washington, D.C. and how everyone cheered him. I remember him saying, "Old soldiers never die, they just fade away." He was really something. Many years later, I had the pleasure of meeting his wife and telling her what an impression that visit made on me. D.C. was my everything; I didn't want to leave it.

But once we arrived in Athens, I loved it. It wasn't the same— we were definitely living on the other side of the tracks there—but it didn't matter to me. As long as I could ride my bike, I was happy.

Soon after arriving in Georgia, I became affiliated with the Athens YMCA and Coburn Kelley. Kelley was my Tom Penrod in Athens, and the YMCA was my D.C. Boys Club. Kelley was larger than life. He was legendary in Athens and still is today. He died in 1968, and now, more than 40 years later, he is being honored with a forthcoming book about his life and influence. The book, authored and edited by Blake Giles, will be a true remembrance of Coburn Kelley. I can't wait to read it.

Poking around on the Internet about Kelley, I came across the following story:

It was the morning of a beautiful, sunny, California day. My daughter, age three and a half, at the time, and I were driving away from her ballet lesson. For conversation sake I had asked her what she wanted to be when she grew up. As expected, she answered like any young girl would upon leaving the ballet lessons she loved. "Daddy," she said, "I want to be a ballerina."

After driving for a few quiet moments the silence was broken by my daughter asking me a question. "Daddy," she said, "when you were a little boy, what did you want to be when you grew up?"

Caught off guard, I fell into pensive thought, and began grappling for an answer. What had I really wanted to be when I grew up? Certainly I should have been able to answer that question. I was 35 years old.

While still deep in thought, my daughter pressed again for the answer. Suddenly, spontaneously, I responded, "I wanted to be like the man I named you after, Coburn F. Kelley. Although taken back by the answer I had just given my daughter, Kelley, I knew it had come directly from the bottom of my heart."

Kelley was special. He gave his life to the YMCA and to so many of us. Everyone growing up around the Y thought he was the greatest. He treated us all the same and he made every single one of us feel special. He died at the young age of 54. He was very important to me, and surely one of the most influential people in my life.

And later, the same man that answered to his daughter when asked what he wanted to be when he grew up, commented,

"It's been 16 years since my daughter asked me the question, 'Daddy, when you were a little boy, what did you want to be when you grew up?' Of all that I know there are few things that I am more certain of than this: I will never be what Coburn Kelley was. No one could. Not only was he the most truly authentic living example of Christ I have ever encountered, but I think I can state with no fear of reprisal that all those who knew him would say the same."

The Athens YMCA swallowed me up in those early times of my youth. I practically lived there. I played all sports and was truly gifted in athletics. I was bigger than most of the kids at the Y and had really developed my skills early. Kelley saw this and would always find a way to even things out for all the boys and the teams. If we were playing a game and had the opponents outmatched, he would have me play guard instead of quarterback, so the game would stay even. That was his way. He was a wonderful man who always strived to make everything fair.

His official title was the physical director of the YMCA in Athens and he ran the Pinetops Camp, which I attended. Everybody—and I mean *everybody*—loved him. He worked with thousand of young boys and became a second father to most. I

Coburn Kelley was inducted into the Athens Athletic Hall of Fame in 2001.

2001 INDUCTEE:
COBURN KELLEY

Coburn Kelley, the longtime legendary Boys Director of the Athens YMCA, and much beloved teacher and mentor to thousands of Athens Youth. He began working at the Y while attending the University of Georgia in 1930. He served the community in this capacity until his death in 1968. He built the Athens Y Camp and Chapel by himself and carried Y boys all over America and Canada by bus. Coburn Kelley was an extremely strong physical man but gentle as a lamb when dealing with youngsters. One of the most famous Athenians of all time, his influence is still felt through the now-adult men he molded. Christian lessons and teachings of Kelley will live forever. Probably the most influential coach/teacher in Athens history.

EVERY DAY IS GAME DAY

respect him for everything he did. I was in great awe of the man and I truly loved him.

The YMCA was one of my memorable stops during the early years of my life along with the famous Varsity Café, where I would take a short respite from my Y activities to get my usual two hot dogs and a coke. It's still there in Athens, just a short distance from its original location.

My love for sports was rescued in Athens and it didn't take long for me to be involved in everything again. We lived in the parsonage next to the church and had a small yard in between where I could play some ball. But it was really in a nearby playground where I brought my alleyway expertise and learned to play quarterback.

My seventh grade teacher, Mae Whatley, and her husband "Big Jim" made sure I kept connected to sports and that I utilized my athletic abilities to the fullest extent. I pitched four no-hitters for Mr. Whatley in Little League baseball and Mrs. Whatley really took me under her wing in the classroom. She was the sweetest lady in the world and they both helped me immensely with my transition. I greatly appreciated what they did for me. They will always mean a lot to me and I will never forget them.

Football, basketball, and baseball continued as the central part of my life. They occupied my time from early morning until late at night. If I wasn't actively involved in some type of game or practice, then I was watching, listening, or thinking about it.

Education was important to me, but mainly because it was something I had to do in order to be able to play sports. By the time I was a freshman in high school, my whole life involved my teams' sports. I was diseased! I have suffered my whole life with Attention Deficit Disorder, which made school difficult for me. I always had very good grades but I had to work hard.

"Football was Francis' third-best sport behind basketball and baseball. He was a tremendous pitcher and shortstop and a great shooting guard."
—CHESTER LEATHERS, LONGTIME FRIEND

I was fortunate enough to have had the ability to play sports at a high level. I was starting on the varsity as a freshman in football, basketball, and baseball at Athens High School.

It didn't matter the sport, I had the ability to see the whole field or court. I have always had a sense about what goes on around me and I believe this was a major factor in my success as an athlete.

Of course, to be successful in athletics, a person must be born with some talent. One has to have the basics. I was very fortunate because God gave me tremendous skills and also gave me a mind to go with them.

I have been told that I was a better basketball player than football player—and I also loved to play baseball—but in the South, football is king. There was no other option in Athens.

My longtime childhood friend Chester Leathers had a major influence on my life, as well as a tremendous impact on my athletic accomplishments. There is no one person who I spent more time with growing up—and competing with—in the neighborhood.

Chester was three years ahead of me in school and a very talented athlete. We were competitive in everything: football, basketball, baseball, golf, whatever piqued our interest at the time. He always brought out the best in me.

The two of us lived it, ate it, devoured it—and it became our existence. We played and competed against each other at everything. We would go to Daytona Beach and play stickball. We would stay out competing at games until 2:00 or 3:00 in the morning. He is a good soul and a wonderful person and he made me a better athlete because of all the competition he gave to me.

"People always say, 'Wow, you played with Fran Tarkenton!' And I say, 'No, I was older; Francis played with me!'"

—CHESTER LEATHERS

In December 2008, I visited my old high school in Athens, now called Clarke Central High School. I had not been back there for many years. I stood at the foul line in our old gym, where Chester once witnessed me sink 113 consecutive free throws during practice. Standing there, it seemed like yesterday, even though it was more than 50 years ago. I took a few shots at the basket. They didn't all go in. Good thing Chester wasn't watching!

At Athens High School, I learned how to play quarterback because of two coaches, Weyman Sellers and Billy Henderson. They were *incredible*. They really taught me the game and the physical rigors necessary to keep in top physical condition and outlast an opponent. Practices were absolutely brutal. Coach Sellers was so tough during our practices that training camp with the Vikings in 1961 and practices at the University of Georgia seemed like napping in the afternoon sun.

We practiced two-a-days in full uniform and gear in the Georgia heat. Practice started with four laps around the field. Coach Sellers would have people in the corners so no one could cut them. Following the laps were calisthenics, 15-yard sprints, and then the dreadful ups and downs. And *then* we would start practice for the day!

I recall the time a player new to Coach Sellers' routines practically sprinted the first lap before practice, thinking the coach had ordered only one lap. The three that followed were almost unbearable for him. He learned early on that Weyman Sellers did things a little bit differently.

Sellers was the head coach and Billy Henderson was the backfield coach. Henderson was a great baseball player during his high school days in Macon, Georgia. These two guys were as hard-nosed as it gets. They were disciplined and knew how to get the best out of their players. They taught me the discipline necessary to play the game properly, even if they almost killed me in the process.

If we lost the game on Friday night, we would scrimmage on Saturday morning for four hours. That was Athens High School football. And Sellers and Henderson were the best at it. Without their teaching and leadership, I might not have continued to play the game or excelled at it. I owe a lot to each of them.

I learned all of the basic game mechanics from my high school coaches. They were pure students of the game and left no stone unturned when it came to funadmentals. The major reason that I rarely fumbled is that they were the ones who taught me how to take the snap from center. They taught me where to stand, where to place my hands. We practiced it over and over and over. They drilled me and drilled me on the snap, which paid dividends throughout my whole career.

It honestly wasn't a lot of fun playing for those guys because it was tough, really tough. It was fundamentals and it was discipline. But after that, playing football at Georgia and for the Vikings was a piece of cake. It was practically effortless compared to what coaches Sellers and Henderson put me through.

We won the Georgia State High School Championship in 1955 with only 25 players on the roster. It was unheard of to accomplish something like that, but we had some great athletes when we defeated Valdosta. We had no B Squad, no freshman team. It was just the 25 of us, and we won it all!

Valdosta High School football in Georgia is like Massillon football in Ohio. Football is everything at Valdosta and the name resonates through the South, synonymous with not just football but winning. It is the most successful high school football program in the United States. The record speaks for itself: 842 wins, 193 losses, and 34 ties—that's a winning percentage of more than 80 percent. A few years ago, Valdosta coach Mike O'Brien told a national audience of coaches that even if Valdosta lost every game for the next 60 years, they would still have a winning percentage.

For us to beat them—and with a squad of only 25 players—was unlikely. But that's just what we did. We won the Georgia State Championship 41–30. My shoulder was separated at the time and I couldn't throw; I threw only one pass in the game and it was incomplete. Instead, we ran the ball, and to much success. We won it on conditioning, fundamentals, and pure discipline, thanks to Coach Sellers and Coach Henderson!

I was a passing quarterback. I could throw the ball 75 yards as a 15-year-old. Earlier that championship season, I separated my shoulder, and I played several games in horrendous pain. As a result of the injury, I compensated by being a conscientious ball handler, which contributed to my success later in my football career. Still, the bad shoulder was with me through my entire high school, college, and professional career. It caused me tremendous discomfort and modified my ability to do many of the things I would like to have done. I played with that bad shoulder for the rest of my career. Fifty-five yards became my maximum.

I never took a day off. Sports engulfed everything I did. I went from football in the fall to basketball in the winter and right into baseball in the spring.

Sometimes, reflecting back on many games and key plays brings me painful memories. I just could not make every throw necessary to make the play successful. Since high school, I have been unable to throw the ball more than 55 yards, and I never threw with intensity after that injury. In compensating for it, I learned how to protect the ball and became comfortable running the bootleg. I adapted by throwing the short pass, running the ball, and keeping control of the football. At the time, I was worried that I might not be able to play college or professional football with the bad shoulder.

I was not a runner in high school or in college, but I relied on my instincts to get me through. I never intended to be a scrambling quarterback in the professional ranks, but that's just what happened. I never lacked the resolve to put forth anything less than an all-out effort to win, whatever it took.

I never took a day off. Sports engulfed everything I did. I went from football in the fall to basketball in the winter and right into baseball in the spring. It never ended and I loved every minute. The tremendous intensity of my involvement never allowed me to have a day of rest for almost 30 years, until I took a knee against the Los Angeles Rams the last game of the 1978 season and retired after 18 years in the National Football League.

I was not a good loser. I had competed and practiced so hard that losing was not acceptable. I recall when we lost in the semifinals of the state baseball championship. I was so sick about the loss that I couldn't go to school the next day. They had to come to my house to get me. I had to be at school or I wouldn't have been allowed to play in the consolation game that afternoon. Sports was my life and winning was the most important part of it.

*   *   *

Now, to the discovery 55 years in the making.

I have worn No.10 throughout my entire career—at Athens High School, as a Georgia Bulldog, and with the Minnesota Vikings, the New York Giants, and the Vikings again when I returned to Minnesota. I chose No. 10 strictly because of Jack Scarbath. When I was growing up in Washington, D.C., he was my hero at the helm of the University of Maryland. The only problem is that Scarbath did *not* wear No. 10 at the University of Maryland—he wore No. 62!

Scarbath wore No. 10 in *high school*. Apparently, when he arrived at the University of Maryland as a freshman, someone took a picture of him in his high school uniform. But he happened to be the 62nd person in line to draw football equipment at U of M, and he was given uniform number 62. (At that time, there were no specific number ranges assigned to positions, so it was not unusual for a quarterback to wear a high number.) I must have seen the high school picture of him somewhere. There were few televisions in the early '50s and even fewer college football broadcasts. I never actually saw him in a Maryland uniform, but I thought I had.

I spoke with Jack recently about how much I idolized him as a kid. We laughed about the mix-up. I only wish I would have told him earlier—like 55 years ago!

*   *   *

As I got closer to graduation, I decided to go to the University of Georgia. It was my home, my local team, and Georgia football was *huge* in the South. Some of my friends and family were surprised by the decision because Georgia already had two great quarterbacks on their roster, Charley Britt and Tommy Lewis, but that was the challenge I wanted. I needed to go to Georgia to see how good I was. And I was about to find out!

CHAPTER 3

Georgia Bulldog Football

"Boys, we are going to make this happen. And I am going to draw out exactly what we are going to do, right here in the dirt."

No one sent me into the game against the University of Texas. No one called out my name saying, "Tarkenton, you're in." I wasn't the starting quarterback for Georgia. In fact, I wasn't even the backup. But I went in the game anyway.

There was never a doubt in my mind that I could play. I just had to convince everyone else of that. During my senior year at Athens High School, as scholarship offers started to come in, it seemed like everyone I knew was asking where I intended to play college football. Many of my friends and acquaintances had expressed concern about me going to the University of Georgia.

Georgia already had two exceptional college quarterbacks in Charley Britt and Tommy Lewis. I heard it time and again: "You won't play!"

Both of them were phenomenal athletes. Of all the players I played with and against, none had the abilities of these two guys. They were big, strong, and could really throw the football—and on top of all that, they could run!

Auburn and Georgia Tech were two of my top choices, but I wanted to go to Georgia more than anything. And most of all, I felt that I needed to know how good I was. I thought if I competed for the quarterback position at Georgia against Britt and Lewis, I would find out very quickly. The Bulldogs had two of the very best quarter-backs in the country right here in Athens, but I wasn't planning to sit on the bench.

I asked myself, "How can I ever be as good as Charley Britt and Tommy Lewis?" But I sincerely believed I had something above their skills and abilities. I figured out how to play and I could make it happen on the football field. I knew that I could run a football team. I got it. I understood the game and I could play! When I went into a Georgia game for the first time, I knew I could take the Bulldogs down the field. I had prepared for it my whole life.

When we opened the 1958 season against Texas, I was not the first-team quarterback in the eyes of the coaches. My name didn't appear first on the depth chart, nor was I announced by the public address announcer or listed in the programs. I wasn't sent into the game as a last-second replacement or as a backup to refresh the offense, either. In fact, the coach had decided that I wasn't even going to play at all that year.

I got into the first game of the season against the Texas Longhorns because I put myself in. I ran onto the field and inserted myself into the lineup as the Georgia quarterback during a third-quarter change of possession. It was just that simple. Much to my surprise—and that of every player on our team—Coach Butts left me in the game.

The SEC is really something. It is an integral part of our history in the South. Teams like Alabama, Auburn, and Georgia have been battling each other since the turn of the 20th century; the pride and passion every bit as intense as the great East Coast rivalries like the Yankees and the Red Sox.

Georgia football is a religion. Within a 300-mile proximity are some of the most sacred college football histories in the nation. Georgia. Auburn. Alabama. Clemson. Florida. Most of the stadiums seat more than 90,000 and every game in the area is televised. Spring scrimmages have drawn as many as 95,000 spectators. As a football player, it is an unbelievable college experience. Words like pageantry, rivalry, alumni, and history don't do justice.

The Georgia Bulldogs are frequently ranked in the top 25 teams in the country. Of course, winning more than 700 college football games has certainly enhanced the history and stoked the fans' passion for victory. The support and loyalty for University of Georgia football is one of pride, honor, and tradition.

The great teams of the '40s solidified that tradition with phenomenal players like Frank Sinkwich and Charley Trippi.

Sinkwich won the 1942 Heisman Trophy, the SEC's first to win the prestigious honor. He came out of Youngstown, Ohio and led the nation in rushing in 1941 under Coach Wally Butts. Sinkwich went on to an NFL career with the Detroit Lions, and in 1944 won the NFL Most Valuable Player Award. He was the Associated Press No. 1 Athlete in 1942 and is in the Georgia Bulldog Circle of Honor and the College Football Hall of Fame.

Georgia football is a religion.

Trippi was another star player for Georgia in the early '40s. He won the Maxwell Award in 1946 and was the Most Valuable Player in the Rose Bowl in 1943 when Georgia beat UCLA 9–0. And as recently as 2007, Charley was ranked No. 20 on ESPN's 25 Greatest Players in College Football. He is in the College Football Hall of Fame, the Georgia Sports Hall of Fame, and still lives in Athens, Georgia. When Bobby Dodd recruited me at Georgia Tech, he told me that he thought Trippi was the greatest college football player of all time.

There is no question Trippi was a great football player at Georgia and with Sinkwich playing in the same era, one can imagine the fervor for Georgia Bulldog football.

When I played at Georgia, the inimitable Pat Dye was there with me. We were good friends. Pat, of course, went on to become a successful coach at (our bitter rival) Auburn. As a Bulldog, Pat was a two time All-American. He played guard and linebacker and was our team captain in 1960. I believe he was one of the greatest college football players of all time. He made more incredible plays on the field than any lineman or linebacker that I have ever seen. He was smart, fast, a fierce competitor, and a loyal friend and teammate. Everyone loved him. I can honestly say that he stands alongside Jim Marshall and Mick Tingelhoff as one of the players for whom I have the absolute highest respect.

Although Dye didn't play the same position, he reminds me of the way the great Pittsburgh Steelers safety Troy Polamalu plays the game, seemingly all over the field.

Dye played in the Canadian Football League for a while before coaching. He coached for nine years with Paul "Bear" Bryant at Alabama, at East Carolina, and Wyoming. His career at Auburn speaks for itself, as one of the greatest coaches who ever lived. He is a member of the College Football Hall of Fame and became an integral part of football in the South.

Another teammate I supremely respect is Bobby Walden, who was an incredible punter. We played for Georgia during the same years and were roommates. In 1958 he led the entire nation in punting and in 1964 led the NFL in punting with a 46.4 yard average. In practice one day, I remember seeing him punt the ball 100 yards with the roll. I have never seen anything like it. It was absolutely unbelievable. Walden punted in the National Football League for 14 years and we played together again from 1964 to 1966 with the Minnesota Vikings. He was also a tremendous runner and receiver and led the Canadian Football League in punting, rushing, and receiving in 1961 and 1962 while playing for the Edmonton Eskimos.

Once in practice, Norm Van Brocklin, our Vikings coach, saw him run some pass patterns and wanted to make him a receiver and running back. Waldon declined; he only wanted to punt.

*   *   *

Getting back to 1958 and my bold decision to enter that season-opening game against Texas…

When I came to Georgia in 1957, freshman players were not eligible to play with the varsity. I had a great freshman season with other first-year players and hoped to play as a regular starter my sophomore year. But Coach Butts saw things differently. Charley Britt was installed as his quarterback and Coach spoke to me about using my sophomore season as a "redshirt" year. (College football programs have an option to allow them to sit out players for a season of play, while allowing them practice time with the team. In essence, it gives the player an extra year of practice and experience.) The plan for me was to complete my freshman year, redshirt my sophomore year, and then have three years of eligibility with the varsity.

I had no interest in being redshirted and I told Coach Butts so. I planned to graduate in four years. Besides, I wanted to play immediately. I was ready!

Coach Butts was a tough one to convince—even after I led our freshman team to a preseason victory over the varsity 14–7. We also beat Clemson, Auburn, and the Georgia Tech freshman teams that fall. I was coming off of a great spring practice and wanted desperately to play my sophomore season.

Butts saw the redshirt year as a good thing for Georgia football and for me. After all, the team had Britt at quarterback and he was really talented. They also had Tommy Lewis. They didn't need to waste a year of my eligibility while I sat around watching those two. There was no hurry from their perspective. I would have to wait.

Wally Butts was legendary. He was the head coach at Georgia from 1939 to 1960 and during that time he won four Southeastern Conference titles, had one undefeated season, and took eight teams to bowl games. There were not as many bowl games then as there are now, so being invited to a bowl was a huge accomplishment.

He won 140 games, lost 86, and tied nine as coach of the Bulldogs. He was a huge advocate of the passing game and was an undisputed leader in bringing that type of offense to SEC football. He was elected to the Georgia Sports Hall of Fame in 1966 and, posthumously, to the College Football Hall of Fame in 1997.

I was impressed with his coaching history, but it didn't intimidate me. I wanted to play. I had worked so hard that summer, determined to show the coaches that I was ready to play my sophomore season. I ran the stadium steps on a regular basis and did everything I could to prepare. And now, with the season ready to begin, I was the third-team quarterback and wasn't in the plans to play even one down the whole year.

We were down 7–0 in the third quarter in Austin and I was standing on the sideline next to Coach Butts saying, "Put me in coach! Put me in the game!" I even went so far as to pull on his coat sleeves to get his attention. He basically ignored me. But I had to do something. I was desperate!

In the third quarter, our defense held Texas and they punted the ball to us. We fair catch the ball and are ready to take possession on our own 5-yard line. I notice that Charley is still sitting on the bench, slow to get up and back onto the field. When I saw that, something just clicked inside me and I went in! I ran out onto the field toward my teammates who were gathered near the end zone.

I entered the huddle and everyone was confused, asking what was going on. I said, "Let's go. We're going down the field."

Coach Butts never said a word. We made a first down, then another, and soon were at midfield. I didn't dare look to the sideline. We continued to make first downs and arrived at the Texas 5-yard line. It became third-and-goal, and I said to the guys in the huddle, "Boys, if we don't get this ball in the end zone, I am going to have to take a bus back to Athens because I am going to be in real trouble!"

So I took the ball from center, did a little scrambling, and hit our receiver in the end zone for a touchdown. We scored! It was unbelievable! I went into the game without permission, and we

marched 95 yards down the field against Texas in Austin, and scored
a touchdown!

It was the first year in college football for the two-point conversion option. I looked over to the sideline and saw our kicker running
onto the field for the extra point try, and I waved him off the field. I
can't believe I did it, but I waved him off, and the team loved it! We
went for the two-point conversion and I found a receiver in the end
zone and we took the lead over Texas 8–7! Back home in Athens, the
town must be going nuts. And here in Texas, the team is going crazy,
and we are beating the Longhorns on their home field!

And I do this by going into the game without the coach's
approval, only to take our team 95 yards down the field for a score.
And then on top of all that, having the audacity to wave our kicker
off the field as we go for two points, to take the lead 8–7 against
Texas, in Austin.

This kind of thing only happens in fairy tales. But it *did* happen
and it was unbelievable. And after 40 years, it is still talked about in
Athens. Sure, it was a crazy thing to do, but I would do it again
without hesitation.

Texas came back in the game by scoring a touchdown, making the
score 14–8. In the next series, Coach Butts put Charley back in at quarterback. I couldn't believe it, but he did. We ended up losing that game
and there was almost a revolt back in Athens, but as the season pro-
gressed, I became the starting quarterback and Charley moved primarily
to defense. The next season, Britt started at quarterback, with Coach
Butts putting me in early in games. I think I took more than 80 percent
of the snaps that season. Charley became a tremendous defensive player
for us and was drafted by the Los Angeles Rams as a defensive back once
he graduated. He was an all-around talented player.

I clearly didn't realize it at the time, but I think you have to have a
great sense of desperation at times to accomplish anything worthwhile.

Because if you don't have that great sense of desperation, then you might never find a way to get it done. If I had accepted what most players would have and simply taken the redshirt year, I may have never played for the Georgia Bulldogs.

I think you have to have a great sense of desperation at times to accomplish anything worthwhile.

There were times after my first game that I wasn't sure I wanted to remain with the team. Coach Butts had done some things that were upsetting to me. If it weren't for Coach Quentin Lumpkin, I probably would not have remained a Bulldog.

Quentin was the son of Jack Lumpkin, who was a professional golfer, Davis Love III's golf coach, and a former quarterback at the University of Georgia. When I came to Georgia, he was the freshman football coach. He came from Macon, Georgia, where he grew up in a really tough neighborhood. He was big, strong, and quiet—a gentle giant. And nobody, and I mean *nobody*, ever messed with Quentin Lumpkin.

He used to go one on one with our big linemen on the freshman team and Coach Lumpkin had no pads on! He was as tough as they come and everyone respected him.

He was critically important to me at the university, and he had a major impact on my life. During my senior year, he took me under his wing and during a very frustrating season made me believe in myself, and convinced me I was a great quarterback.

During my sophomore year after the Texas game, Coach Butts was playing me some of the time and Britt at other times. I was confused and frustrated. Butts was enamored with Britt, who was the bigger, faster, and stronger quarterback, yet I felt that I was the one who should be playing.

I was a strongly religious kid back then and didn't swear, smoke, or drink. One day on the practice field, Butts lit into Walden with a profanity-laced tirade. That was it for me. Enough was enough and I was prepared to quit the team.

That evening in the dormitory, Pat Dye, center Phil Ashe, tailback Bill "Taterbug" Godfrey, and I all decided we were going to leave the university. I had told everyone, "Boys, I'm leaving. I am not staying here." And one by one, they joined me. Pat's older brother was the team captain, he caught wind of our plan and went to Coach Butts. It wasn't long before we were summoned to see Coach at his home in Athens. After the meeting, we returned to the dormitory and talked it over. Nothing the coach had said had made us change our minds.

So we went up to Phil's house in Stone Mountain, Georgia to figure out what we were going to do. We were all very key players to the team, and especially next year's team. Our plan was to call Florida State the next morning and transfer there. All of a sudden, there came a knock on the door. It was Quentin Lumpkin. And at that point, we knew it was all over. He is the only man that could have gotten the four of us to stay at Georgia. He didn't have to say a single word. We all loved him and his presence was enough. All he had to do was walk in the door and our plans floated away.

Coach Lumpkin never berated us or criticized us for what we had done; he just told us to come back. He didn't even have to say that. We all respected him so much that we did.

After that episode, I began to play as the quarterback and things got much better. I owe Coach Lumpkin for his intervention and for all the many things he did for me. He was critical to my life and to my success. He was always there for me and never had an agenda, just his goodwill. He came to my father's funeral and when I saw him there, I told him that I loved him and I truly did. He told me he loved me too, and it means so much.

Overall, I loved playing football for the University of Georgia. I had a good time and we had fun—especially in the huddles. I always tried to make it interesting. People have said that I used to draw plays in the dirt right on the field. Well, that's absolutely true. I did it in the pro ranks, as well.

One of the great moments in the history of Georgia football, and certainly in my career there, happened in 1959. We had been picked to finish 10th in our 12-team conference. But our team came together, and we ended up playing against our archrival Auburn in the second-to-last game of the season, for the SEC Championship.

Auburn was a true powerhouse team at the time with three All-Americans in Jackie Burkett, Zeke Smith, and Ken Rice.

But we came out and gave them an historic defensive battle. We played our hearts out in the game, and came down to the last few minutes of play with us down by a score of 13–7. Our only score came on a punt return for a touchdown by Charley (who had earlier in the year scored on a 100-yard interception, which became the critical play in our victory against Florida.)

With just a few minutes remaining in the game, Auburn fumbled near its 45-yard line and Pat recovered the ball for us. On the first three plays we miss—and then on fourth down I hit Don Soberdash for a first down, and we're off and running. I completed a second pass to Don and we make another first down. The drive stalls on the 13-yard line, and we have fourth down facing us. We have one play, and a field goal won't do it. We don't have a play, so we call a time out.

We had plenty of good times in those Georgia huddles. They were interactive, we laughed, and we always had fun. But this was serious business. This was for the conference championship and we had one play to make it happen. I said to the team, "Boys, we are going to make this happen, and I am going to draw out exactly what we are going to do, right here in the dirt."

Back in those says, there was no such thing as split ends. Ends were on the end of the line. I started drawing in the dirt, "I am going to roll out to the right. You all need to do your normal blocking and I want everyone to block your man to the right. We want them to think we are going to run a roll pass option to the right side of the field. And we need to sell it to them. Now, Bill [Herron], I want you to block down on your man and count to four—*one thousand one*, and don't you cheat on me. Take the full second on that count and then when you hit four, run to the left corner of the end zone and look over your left shoulder for the ball. The ball is going to be there and you are going to catch it for a touchdown!"

So I rolled out to the right, the blocking was perfect, and I started the count, *one thousand one, one thousand two, one thousand three, one thousand four*, and I stopped and threw the ball to the left corner of the end zone. Bill was wide open and we scored the touchdown. The entire place and the sideline went crazy. The score was tied 13–13 and we need the extra point to win the championship.

Durward Pennington, our great kicker from Albany, Georgia, will absolutely deny this, but I remember every single detail about that historic game—and I have my teammates to confirm the story. Pennington took the field and put himself in position as he had done in so many games before. He calmly kicked the extra point, and we win the game.

Everyone went nuts again! Georgia has won the championship! Durward ran to the sideline and I'm hugging him and the team's smothering him and he looked at me with a puzzled expression and asked me why everyone was acting that way when we already had the game won. He didn't know that the game was on the line! Can you imagine? He had no idea that the score was tied and he needed to win it with the kick! I think he almost fainted when I told him.

We beat Auburn on that championship day, and it was a great win for Georgia football and all the fans, alumni, coaches, and players. Perhaps the best part of it all was the fact that the game-winning play was drawn up in the dirt.

*　　*　　*

Georgia football was always very special to me. I loved my teammates and reveled in the competition for the quarterback position with Charley Britt and Tommy Lewis. Despite our rivalry, both became great friends of mine. Although Lewis never played much at the quarterback position, he became our biggest cheerleader. He was a wonderful person and an incredible teammate. He became a fighter pilot and later a flight instructor. Charley, of course, went on to a career with the Los Angeles Rams and the Minnesota Vikings.

I was proud to play for the Bulldogs and proud of my achievements. I owe a lot to the university, the fans, coaches, and my teammates. It was frontline college football and I was enthralled by it. Professional football was waiting and I was ready for the challenge.

My dreams for the future were to play in the National Football League with my team of past heroes, the Washington Redskins. Little did I know, I would soon be dressed in purple and wearing horns on the side of my head.

CHAPTER 4

Drafted By Who?

I had never heard of the Vikings! I didn't even know who they were!

When I was drafted in the third round of the 1961 NFL Draft by the Minnesota Vikings, I had no idea who they were.

I had been in Montgomery, Alabama practicing for the Blue-Gray game with Norm Snead. We were the quarterbacks for the Gray squad that year and Norm and I became good friends.

Norm was rewarded for his great college career at Wake Forest by being drafted in the first round of the NFL Draft by the Washington Redskins, the second player taken in the draft that year. I thought *I* was going to be playing for the Redskins. I had even been told that George Preston Marshall, the Washington owner, was going to draft me. Unfortunately, it didn't happen. The Minnesota Vikings drafted me in the third round and I was shocked. I had never heard of the Vikings! I didn't know who they were!

The Vikings at the time were only a concept; there was no team. The NFL owners had awarded the Twin Cities with an NFL franchise that would start play in the 1961 season. So not only was I playing for a franchise that I had never heard of, but I had no teammates. Not only that, but I was drafted in the third round. As a quarterback, if you are drafted in the third round, the team is sending you a message. That message?: *You are not good enough, big enough, fast enough, or strong enough to play the game. If you were, you would have been drafted earlier.* It wasn't the message I wanted to hear going into my rookie season.

But I didn't worry. It wouldn't be long before the Minnesota Vikings and the other National Football League teams would find out that I could play the game, and play it very well. I was determined to prove that my position in the draft would have no bearing on my success as an NFL quarterback. And my determination, without question, prevailed. I played for 18 years.

One of the original owners and key influences in securing a franchise for Minnesota was Max Winter. Max's incredible passion for the game of football drove him to begin a crusade to bring professional football to the Midwest, and to the Twin Cities in particular. With the assistance of Chicago Bears owner George Halas, the league granted the Twin Cities a franchise in January of 1960, to begin play in the fall of 1961. Halas was an NFL icon and a force among owners. When he said he wanted the Minnesota Vikings to be in the National Football League, people listened. (Some thought that the American Football League should grant the franchise to Minnesota, but Halas insisted that the NFL be the home of the Vikings, and he eventually prevailed.) I'm sure he anticipated the rivalry that would develop between the new team and his Bears, which were only 400 miles away. It came about almost instantaneously.

This newly formed team, with its unusual mix of players and personalities dressed in purple with horns on the side of the helmets, came together in its newly anointed city, and thanked the great Bears leader by soundly beating his Chicago Bears to open the 1961 season. Not only was the loss a crushing blow to the "Papa Bear," but it was perhaps the most devastating defeat in their storied history.

I will challenge anyone to go against my belief that the 1961 season opener between the Minnesota Vikings and the Chicago Bears was the greatest upset in the history of the league. For the Vikings to prevail in this historic debut by the score of 37–13 was nothing short of preposterous.

Not only were we a brand-new team, but we had lost all five exhibition games in the preseason. Just two weeks earlier, we had played the Bears before 5,000 fans in Cedar Rapids, Iowa, and got absolutely killed! It was awful. They were the Chicago Bears, the Monsters of the Midway, and we weren't anywhere near their caliber. It was the mismatch of all mismatches! And they were to be our opening game opponents.

The Bears were the mold for professional football. Their great players and teams of the past were synonymous with tradition. After all, they had been playing in Chicago since 1921! They had won NFL Championships, had a record number of wins, and boasted many Hall of Fame inductees—players like Red Grange and Bronko Nagurski. And to top it all off, they had Halas, who had been running the Bears operations for more than 40 years.

In essence, we got the players that the other teams felt couldn't play.

Halas took over in 1920 and moved the club from Decatur, Illinois, to Chicago, renaming them the Bears. And he had been with them ever since, winning NFL Championships in 1921, 1932, 1933, 1940, 1941, 1943, 1946—and were about to win another in 1963. Halas purchased the rights to the team for $100 and built them into a dynasty.

The Vikings, on the other hand, were a collection comprised of a bunch of other teams' castoffs. When the league expanded, each team was permitted to protect 30 players on its roster. The rest were up for grabs for the Vikings to consider. In essence, we got the players that other teams felt couldn't play, plus the guys chosen in the 1961 draft.

That's where I came in, along with guys like Tommy Mason, Hugh McElhenny, Bill Bishop, and Don Joyce. Mason was a collegiate running back from Tulane University, and the others were great players from years back.

I was comfortable at Georgia. I was an All-American in 1960, and knew I could play professional football, even though most of the NFL had its doubts. So I left my home in Athens, Georgia, and drove to a little town called Bemidji, Minnesota, for Vikings training camp. I soon realized Minnesota was where I was supposed to be. Minnesota was a good fit for me and I loved playing for the Vikings.

When I arrived at Vikings training camp, George Shaw, a seasoned veteran from the Baltimore Colts and New York Giants, was there and it was understood that he would be the starting quarterback. Including me, we had *six* quarterbacks trying to make the opening day roster. OK, so Shaw was going to be the starting quarterback. But I knew that I was going to play. I could throw the ball and I could make things happen on the field. There was absolutely no doubt in my mind that I was going to make the team.

There was absolutely no doubt in my mind that I was going to make the team.

When I look back on that time, I often think how audacious I was to be so confident. Who was I to think that I was going to make the Minnesota Vikings professional football team as a rookie quarterback? But I did think so, and I never had a second thought about it. If I had not earned a position on the team, I don't know what I would have done. It was all I had prepared for in my life. I had no other plans. Failure was not an option for me.

I remember the first scrimmage in training camp. I was getting killed, but I got through it. I was confident in my talent and my ability to lead the team; I had to overcome thoughts that I was playing on a team with little chance to win. The previous year, Dallas had been granted a franchise and finished the season 0–11–1. One tie—that was it. As the new expansion team, what were our chances going to be? None! We had absolutely *no* chance! Our future looked grim, to say the least.

Still, I had hope. During the last game of our exhibition season against the Los Angeles Rams, I was beginning to "get it" to some extent. I was learning more about the professional game each week, and I was starting to get a feel for the game and was gaining confidence. I knew that God had given me this talent, and I also knew that he had given me the sense to understand the game. I had a strong desire to learn, and as each game went by, I understood it more. Coach Norm Van Brocklin was instrumental in teaching me the professional game. And even though we had our differences for many years, I give him great credit and appreciate what he taught me.

But now it was crunch time. I knew who the Minnesota Vikings were. I had been with them since the beginning of training camp and several exhibition games. I was ready for the season to begin and ready to start my career in the NFL.

CHAPTER 5

Monsters of the Midway

The Vikings were born and came immediately to life that Sunday against the Bears.

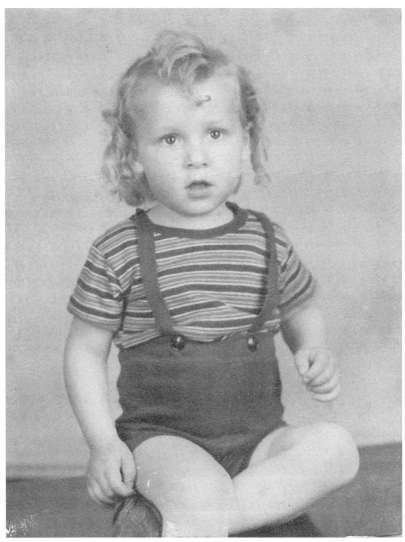

Francis Asbury Tarkenton, born February 3, 1940. (Photo courtesy of the Tarkenton family)

The house on 5th Street, N.W. in Washington, D.C. (Photo courtesy of the Tarkenton family)

My father's church in Washington, D.C. (Photo courtesy of the Tarkenton family)

My dad (second from left) was a preacher. That's me, second from right. (Photo courtesy of the Tarkenton family)

I may have been a cowboy as a boy, but I grew up to be a Viking. (Photo courtesy of the Tarkenton family)

Coburn Kelley was an incredible influence and role model not just to me, but to generations of boys growing up in Athens, Georgia. (Photo courtesy of the Tarkenton family)

Sports, from the time I could first breathe, were my life. (Photo courtesy of the Tarkenton family)

My family (left to right): Dallas, my mother, father, and me. My brother Wendell is in front. (Photo courtesy of the Tarkenton family)

Georgia had two great quarterbacks in Charley Britt and Tommy Lewis. I thought if I competed for the quarterback position at Georgia against Britt and Lewis, I would find out very quickly how good I really was. (Photo courtesy of Getty Images)

A headshot of me at the University of Georgia (Photo courtesy of the Tarkenton family)

George Halas was instrumental in bringing the National Football League to Minnesota. (Photo courtesy of Patrick McCaskey)

We thanked Halas by shellacking his Chicago Bears in our inaugural game, 37–13. I threw four touchdown passes and ran for another. (Photo courtesy of the Minnesota Vikings)

Norm Van Brocklin was a master of the game plan.
(Photo courtesy of Getty Images)

Three early Minnesota quarterbacks (left to right): Ron Vander Kelen, me, and John McCormick.
(Photo courtesy of the Minnesota Vikings)

I will be the first to admit that Norm Van Brocklin and I never hit it off. Our personalities were very different, and the way we interacted with others was at opposite extremes. He was a terrific quarterback in the National Football League for a long time, and he taught me the intricate details of the professional game, but I often thought that he had a strange way of doing things.

The week before the first game of the inaugural season for the Minnesota Vikings, Norm invited my wife and me to his house. He told me I was going to start at quarterback against the Chicago Bears that coming Sunday. I was his first-year rookie quarterback, and he was giving me the reins.

All he said was, "Kid, you're in." It was simple and it was direct. That was it. The job was mine! I was the number-one starter! I remember the exhilaration that I felt.

I never had a doubt about my ability to make the team or about my belief that I was going to be a quarterback in the National Football League. But this was big. I was going to start in my first game, and for the Vikings' first regular season game. It was one for the history books.

I looked around me at his big house and nice cars and thought to myself, *this is what I can be and what I can have.* My hard work and dedication was paying off. This could be my future.

I was just beginning to comprehend the passing game at the professional level, but I had the basics in tow. But for a rookie quarterback starting in my first game, I felt as though I was well prepared. And then the bubble burst. On Sunday morning before the game, Van Brocklin came up to me and said, "I am going to start George Shaw today. I thought it over, and he is a veteran player. He deserves it."

I was devastated. It was such a startling blow that I'm not sure our relationship was ever the same. I had gone from the starting quarterback to the bench without ever stepping onto the field.

So Shaw started the game, and things did not go well from the onset. It didn't take long for Van Brocklin to change his mind again. I went into the game early in the first quarter and I never came out. The game was a *huge* victory for us, and it set the tone for my career in the NFL. There I was, a 21-year-old kid, playing quarterback for the Minnesota Vikings. The reality of it was, I wasn't just ready to go into the game, I was ready to *play* the game.

I had lived and breathed the game my whole life. From the time I was throwing footballs to my brother, Dallas, in the alleys of Washington, D.C., I thought of nothing else. So when Van Brocklin put together the game plan and laid out all the variables and possibilities, it was clear to me. Even though I was a rookie, I understood my role as quarterback. My high school coaches had taught me well. As I became a more seasoned player and compiled years of experience, I developed my understanding of the passing game even further.

I love what they have been doing at Texas Tech recently. Coach Mike Leach never played college football, and yet the team has become revolutionary in its passing game. Leach is a guy with a law degree who wanted to become a college football coach, and he has truly gone after it. He knows more about the passing game than most college coaches. He has studied it and worked at it. And he knocked off mighty Texas in the fall of 2008 because of his grasp of the game.

If one studies the game for long enough, he can learn plenty. One of the most important things I learned about throwing the football was never to force a quick throw. I wanted to make every throw easy; this was always foremost in my mind. It was a key ingredient to my success.

If you are playing golf and you have a 50-foot putt to the hole, you are going to three putt most of the time, aren't you? Whereas, if you have a one-foot putt, you are going to make it most of the time.

It's the same way with throwing the football. The best passing schemes are the ones with easy throws. Van Brocklin designed a game plan against the Bears and I relished in the concept.

When Bill Walsh was coaching the 49ers in San Francisco, he had his quarterbacks make easy throws. Joe Montana, one of the best quarterbacks to play the game, made easy throws over and over. Those who followed in Walsh's West Coast offensive scheme, like Steve DeBerg and Steve Young, who were successful quarterbacks for many years, made the same easy throws time and again.

Today, everyone seems to be impressed by the "big arm" quarterbacks who can throw the ball down the field at long distances. But the real question is, how many completions are they making, and how difficult are the catches by the receivers?

Anytime a quarterback is put in a position to have to make a great throw in order to get a completion, there is something wrong with the system. It doesn't matter how strong a quarterback's arm is, or how far he can throw it down the field, or at what speed. It should be about putting the player in a position to make a high-percentage throw. A 40-yard pass down the field can be a good play, but it must be set up by short, easy passes to be effective.

Going into the game, I had a specific game plan in mind. I recognized the Bears' blitz defense. I knew what was coming and was prepared for it. Of course, it's one thing to recognize the defense and have a plan, and yet another thing to have that plan work. Well, on this particular Sunday, it worked. Never once in the game did I have to make a hard throw or a difficult decision. Van Brocklin's game strategy was absolutely impeccable. Everything we did that day worked to perfection. It was the Dutchman's understanding of the game that brought us to victory. Maybe it was all supposed to be that way that day. The Vikings were born and came immediately to life that Sunday against the Bears.

Van Brocklin was a brilliant field general. He knew how to put together a game plan and he knew how to attack the opponent. And he knew how to teach me. He taught me how to prepare and how to understand the passing game. If Van Brocklin put together a game plan, I felt that if I was able to execute it to perfection, we would never lose a game. He was that good. He had the purest understanding of what needed to be done on the football field from the quarterback perspective as anyone I've ever known. He learned it from Sid Gillman, who got it from others, and he taught me to learn from other greats of the game who were successful as well.

Learning from quarterbacks of the past who had excelled at what they did was the way I developed. I was a sponge, and at this time in my life, I soaked up everything Van Brocklin had to say. Later, I would learn from Y.A. Tittle and Sid Luckman and coaches Jerry Burns and Bud Grant, all of whom helped me immensely.

Coach Van Brocklin put me into the game early on, and it proved to be a good decision. I passed for four touchdowns and ran in another. I consider it the greatest win of my career; the transverse of that terrible game in Dallas. That first victory against the Bears was a high among highs and a tribute to all my Viking teammates, who everyone said had no chance to win that day.

> *"Francis learned a lot from Van Brocklin and really learned to read defenses. He would literally draw up plays in the dirt during games."*
>
> —Fred Cox,
> former Minnesota Vikings kicker

We played our hearts out, and even though we crushed Halas' Bears, it was still a thank you to him for bringing us into the NFL. It was a tremendous victory, no question about that.

The true heart and soul, and the cornerstone of the Minnesota Vikings team, were set in place that day.

It took a full year before some of the franchise's earliest heroes like Mick Tingelhoff and Grady Alderman started to arrive. But there was one man already here and he would stay for 19 seasons. And no one wore the purple colors more proudly than Jim Marshall. Marshall is a special player. There is no one person in this world like him. Jim means a lot to me, and he has meant a lot to the Minnesota Vikings, too.

> *"Fran always put the team first. He was never willing at any time to give up on a play."*
> —GRADY ALDERMAN, FORMER MINNESOTA VIKING TACKLE

Jim was a great athlete and as smart a player as I have ever played with or against. We used to play chess and I could never beat him—he always won. And he always brought his A game with him on Sundays. I believe I can challenge anyone intellectually, but I tried many times to top Jim and I never could. Whether it was a game of chess or an argument about virtually anything, Jim was the best. I could never get that step ahead of him.

Jim had played in Cleveland the previous year, and had gotten ill and lost a lot of weight. He arrived at the Vikings weighing just 215 pounds—and he was going up against the likes of Jim Parker from Baltimore who weighed 280! The Browns had cut him in camp, and he had come to us a week later. Can you imagine that? The Browns didn't think that he could play! I would not have liked to have been the person who pulled the trigger on that decision.

Jim never had a bad game. We were at opposite ends of the locker room and his passion and desire just exuded across the room. I admired him so much. He played in 282 consecutive games, 270 of them with the Vikings! Just think of that, 282 games over 20 years in the National Football League and he isn't in the Hall of Fame? It's criminal! It was a great privilege, honor, and wonderful experience to have had the opportunity to watch Jim Marshall play the game. And to call him my teammate and friend will always be very special to me.

It was an extraordinary group of Vikings that formed the nucleus that would ascend to future greatness. In the early years, a few more arrived and the foundation of the franchise was cemented. Players like Mick Tingelhoff, Grady Alderman, Bill Brown, Dave Osborn, Fred Cox, Carl Eller, and many others started something memorable.

The great Bears player and former head coach Mike Ditka told me a while back that he was in the Twin Cities and had the opportunity to see some of the old Purple greats. He saw the connection they had to one another and told me they never had in Chicago what the old Vikings have today, an enduring friendship after all these years. It's a special bond and it always will be.

> "What a tremendous thrill he always gave us!"
>
> —Don Mooney, a fan for life

The Vikings were fortunate to have several exceptional players who arrived around the same time, played for several years, were very successful winning championships, and now all live in the area. It is wonderful for them, the franchise, and the community.

So the 1961 season began with our surprise defeat of the Chicago Bears, and the legacy lives on today. I think about the Bears game and that victory all the time. It was the day a group of rookies, cast-offs, and players no one else wanted on their rosters did the impossible and defeated the Monsters of the Midway. It remains one of the great moments of my life.

Chapter 6

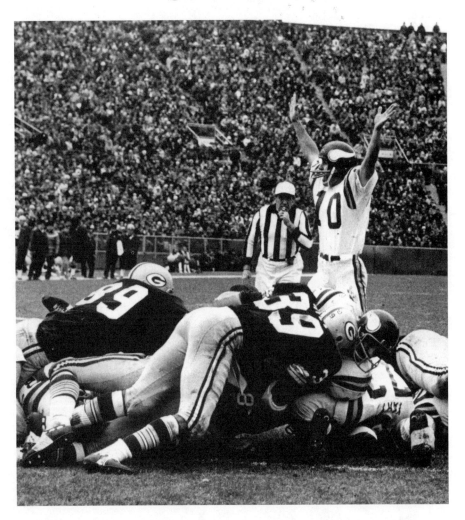

Early Years in Purple

They may have been the greatest collection of characters that I have ever been around in all my football playing years.

They may have been the greatest collection of characters that I have ever been around in all of my football playing years. I remember them as much as any group I have ever been associated with.

They were a part of the Minnesota Vikings football club from 1961 to 1966, the years I spent with the team before I was traded to the New York Giants. And they were characters! They came from everywhere—other teams, as draft choices, as free agents, and from right off the street. Some would call them misfits because they didn't fit the plans of other clubs, or cast-offs because they were cut, released, or waived from the rosters of other teams. Whatever they were called, they were a group like no other ever assembled.

Some had been tremendous players of the past and were left unprotected on the rosters of NFL teams. Players like Don Joyce from the Baltimore Colts and Bill Bishop of the Bears—good players for many years who were looking for a place to continue their careers. Many had been impact players with their other teams and were recognized for their accomplishments. In addition, all these young kids like me were thrown in with the veterans. It was a unique experience for all of us. And every day was interesting and exciting.

We were fortunate enough to have "the King," Hugh McElhenny, on our team in 1961. He was one of the greatest running backs to have ever played the game. I could not understand how the 49ers could have made the decision to let him go. But I was happy to have him there with the rest of us.

To have had the opportunity to be around these aged veterans like Joyce, Bishop, McElhenny, and others, and to observe their passion and skill firsthand, was something to behold.

But with all these characters, new and old, our setting was *Animal House*. We had guys like Bill "Stray Dog" Lapham, who got his name from Van Brocklin because he said he was always looking for someone to block, but could never find his man. There was something new and dramatic going on every day. And there I was in the middle of the whole thing. It made for great memories and I wouldn't trade it for anything.

I was a preacher's kid, without a worldly bone in my body, and those old grizzled veterans showed me the way. They were gruff and they were big, and some had been around the league for more than a decade. I was still throwing footballs in the alleys of Washington D.C. when some of my teammates began their professional careers.

One of my first recollections, and a fitting way to welcome me to professional football, was being put in imminent danger with the likes of the great 49ers legend Leo Nomellini. He was a two-time All-American at the University of Minnesota and played for the San Francisco 49ers for 14 seasons. He was the 49ers first draft pick in 1950 and was ultimately elected to the Pro Football Hall of Fame. This guy played in 10 Pro Bowls, was selected to the All-Pro NFL Team six times, twice on offense and four times on defense—an All-Pro player on both sides of the ball—and he was named to the NFL's All Time Team as a defensive tackle. And to make matters even worse for me, in the off-season, he was professional wrestler "Leo the Lion," a World Wrestling Champion and a World Wrestling Tag Team Champion. I was no match for him.

We were playing San Francisco in an exhibition game and I had been warned by some of our veterans about Nomellini. They said he had a glass eye or something and he looked terrifying. So I went to the King, who had played with Leo for years, and asked his advice. He said gravely, "Kid, let me tell you something. When you get in the game, do yourself a huge favor. Nomellini is going to be right there in front of you. *Don't look at him*, because he will scare you to death!"

So my plan was to not look at him. Van Brocklin puts me into the game and tells me if I hear someone grunting, it's Nomellini. "He grunts when he runs." So I couldn't look at him or listen for him.

But I can't help myself—I just *have* to look at him. So I do, and it was terrible! I think he had that eye in the middle of his forehead. He looked like a Cyclops and he scared me to death! These kind of mythical things made it all so different from anything I had experienced in my past. These guys were light years older than me. They had grown up in the game and were seasoned veterans of the gridiron.

Playing alongside them helped define who I was as a player and as a man. I had never experienced anything like those early Viking teams. But all of them were characters among characters. There were great players of the past, great players of the future, good players, not-so-good players, fair players, and mediocre players, all making up the training camp roster of the Vikings in the early '60s.

Hugh McElheny drove a Cadillac and always wore all black. He looked like a movie star—and what an incredible football player he was! He was charming, smart, and was truly "the King."

We had also Dave Middleton—actually, *Dr.* Dave Middleton—from Auburn. He used to arrive to training camp late because he was in medical school at the University of Michigan. He was a wonderful wide receiver, and gifted in many ways.

Jerry Reichow could really catch the football. He stayed with the Vikings organization for almost 50 years. Bob Schnelker was also there in the early days; he later coached with Jerry Burns when he became the Vikings head coach.

The middle of our defense was anchored by a character named "Rip" Hawkins, who was my roommate my first year. He was a good person and a great middle linebacker, but he did not have a burning interest in the game. He retired after playing only five years. He had tremendous ability and did a fantastic job for us. I wish he had played longer.

One of our early offensive linemen was Larry Bowie from Purdue. Larry was not recognized for being as good as he was. He was rock solid and tough as nails. He had a big ol' smile and never said a whole lot, but he was a rugged, hard-nosed football player.

"Red" Phillips was injured when he came to us, so he never played much, but he was a fine receiver. We were lucky to have had him, if only for a short time.

There were so many others in those early years that I have fond memories of being around—players like Clancy Osborne, Charlie Sumner, Karl Rubke, and Ed "Bozo" Sharockman, to name a few.

Our team back then was trying to find our identity because we didn't have one. Everyone was from somewhere else, including Van Brocklin, who had never been a coach before. In many respects he was still a player.

In those early days, we had no stability. Players were coming and going and we had a hard time forming any consistency. Common ground came to us in the form of two people: Fred Zamberletti, our trainer, and our equipment manager "Stubby" Eason. They kept everything calm, and helped us get through all of the early drama. From the get-go, Zamberletti was everybody's best friend. He had absolutely no enemies. Fred would tape our ankles and talk a blue streak, waving his arms and hands wildly, telling stories. He understood the players and knew how to keep us level. He and Stubby were the two "rocks" of the franchise. We could always depend on them and they were always there for us. They were two people we could lean on. We might see our best friend on the team leave the next day; times were turbulent. We didn't know what was going to happen next. We were never quite sure of Van Brocklin's agenda. We didn't know who we were as a football team—and it was that way for the first several years.

A number of the great Viking leaders and players of the future arrived in the early to mid-'60s. Mick Tingelhoff, Grady Alderman, Jim Marshall, Carl Eller, Bill Brown, Fred Cox, Dave Osborn, Paul Flatley, and others began to provide some of the missing stability to the rest of us. Players were still coming and leaving but the team was starting to solidify.

In 1965, our middle linebacker position was defined with the emergence of Lonnie Warwick out of Tennessee Tech. Lonnie played with the Vikings from 1965 to 1972. He brought a palpable physical toughness to our defense, and was the player that defined who we were when our opponents were in possession of the ball. He catalyzed our team's hard-nosed defensive football. He was our Ray Nitschke and our Dick Butkus.

Warwick played for eight years and was part of our great linebacking core with Roy Winston, and later Wally Hilgenberg. They were a formidable trio on the field, and great friends to boot. They wore numbers 58, 59, and 60.

> *"Francis Tarkenton was the best quarterback I have ever seen play the game."*
> —DAVE OSBORN, FORMER RUNNING BACK, MINNESOTA VIKINGS.

Hilgenberg was number 58, Warwick 59, and Winston was 60. Starting from the right side, they lined up: 58, 59, and 60. When they hunted together, they sat in the truck in order. When Wally Hilgenberg was 58 years old, Warwick was 59 years old, and Winston was 60. And, to top it all off, Hilgenberg's initials are W.W.H, Winston, Warwick, and Hilgenberg! The three of them have quite a legacy. It was a hard loss for the community and the Vikings organization when Hilgenberg passed away in 2008 from Lou Gehrig's Disease. He was a tough and passionate player, as were Warwick and Winston.

Gary Larsen came to the Vikings in the mid-'60s and stayed for ten years. He was a terrific player but was always overshadowed by the greatness of Marshall, Eller, and Page, who arrived with the Vikings after I had left for New York. Page was an incredible player and his presence made Eller and Marshall even better than they already were. Together with Gary Larsen, the legendary Purple People Eaters were formed.

The defining parts of the team were coming together as the franchise grew with experience. Players like Karl Kassulke and Dale Hackbart brought further toughness and credibility to the defense, while the tandem of Dave Osborn and Bill Brown was among the best to carry the ball in the same backfield.

Just as I was getting comfortable with my teammates and friends, other variables resulted in me leaving for New York. I hated to leave the Vikings but the possibility of playing there any longer was not in the cards.

And then Harry Peter "Bud" Grant came in to take over the Vikings as the head coach in 1967, the same year that I left. I was in New York but got full reports from my friends on the Vikings. The stories passed on to me across the country were incredible. Grant and Van Brocklin were absolute polar opposites; Grant was different in his approach to everything. He had them standing at attention for the National Anthem—and they practiced it!

It didn't take long for the players to start believing that Bud had it all figured out, and knew what he was doing. They didn't win much in their first year under Grant, but the wins came soon enough.

However, my path took me in another direction: the New York Giants.

CHAPTER 7

Traded to the Big Apple

I had made up my mind. I was not going back for the 1967 season, and that was final.

I absolutely loved playing in Minnesota and I loved my teammates. But it was time for me to move on.

There is no question in my mind that Norm Van Brocklin taught me the game of professional football. He was a brilliant strategist and he could put together a game plan better than anybody. But after six seasons together, it was time to go. Our relationship, pure and simple, did not work. I was miserable. And so I came to the decision that my days with the Minnesota Vikings were over.

One thing I have learned about myself through the years is that when I decide something is over, it's over, and there is no turning back. And I knew my relationship with Van Brocklin and the Minnesota Vikings had come to an end. I had made up my mind I was not going back for the 1967 season, and that was final.

It was around the end of January or early February of that year when I called Jim Finks, Vikings general manager, and asked for a meeting. I flew up to the Twin Cities but was intercepted by Van Brocklin at the Vikings' offices. I never got that meeting with Finks. Instead, Van Brocklin and I talked for some time. He made every effort to smooth things over and try to resolve the issues. But I was direct with him, and made it clear in no uncertain terms that I would not play for the Minnesota Vikings again.

I told him that I was only 26 years old and that I continued to see a future for myself in professional football, but not with the Vikings. I have always judged people in my life on what they say and what they do, and there had been too many problems in this regard with Norm to see any resolution on the horizon. I told him that if the Vikings didn't trade me to another team, I would retire.

Not long after I arrived back home to Atlanta, I received a phone call from Jim Finks. He said he was very glad to hear that Norm and I had put our differences behind us and worked things out. He said he was looking forward to my return for the 1967 season.

I couldn't believe it. I told Jim that I had made it clear to Van Brocklin that I was not coming back to the Vikings, and that they should trade me or I would retire from football. Finks was shocked; he had gotten a different message.

In order to be resolute, my lawyer advised me to write the following letter to Jim Finks:

> *Dear Norm,*
>
> *After much thought, I have come to a definite conclusion that under no circumstances can I return to play football with the Minnesota Vikings next season.*
>
> *Because of the events of the past few months and my feelings toward a number of things, it is impossible for me to return to the Vikings with a clear and open mind. As you know I have tried to subdue these feelings and erase them from my mind, but it has been impossible.*
>
> *Feeling as I do, I am sure this decision is the best for the Vikings, you, and myself.*
>
> *Norm, I sincerely appreciate your help and guidance during the early years of my pro career and I certainly wish for you, and the Vikings, every success.*
>
> *I hope you and the organization understand that nothing can be done that would change my decision.*
>
> *Because of all that the organization has done for me, I am writing this letter in the event that it might be helpful to the Vikings to know my feelings at this time.*
>
> *Sincerely,*
>
> *Francis A. Tarkenton*

Soon after the letter arrived, it got in the hands of the media and received national exposure. Jim Finks and Bernie Ridder, one of the

Vikings owners, called me in Atlanta, asking to meet with me in Chicago to discuss the situation. They told me that their plan was to fire Van Brocklin and they wanted me to remain with the Vikings. I told them I wanted absolutely no part of it. I had no intention of returning to the Vikings, especially if it meant firing Van Brocklin. No matter what their grounds, that dismissal would always be linked to my desire to leave the organization and I refused to be connected with it.

"When he was traded to the New York Giants in 1967, I wasn't sure I wanted to keep playing without him."

—Grady Alderman

I had made my decision to leave based on many factors; I did not want to leverage Van Brocklin out the door. I didn't want that to be my legacy in Minnesota. No, my decision was final, and the Vikings needed to trade me. Two days later Van Brocklin resigned. And not too long after all this drama, it was announced in Gotham that they had obtained a quarterback from the Minnesota Vikings named Francis Asbury Tarkenton.

*   *   *

There is such incredible tradition associated with the New York Giants. I grew up in love with the Washington Redskins and Sammy Baugh, but I was certainly aware of the Giants and many of their legendary players like Kyle Rote, Frank Gifford, Charlie Conerly, and the great Y.A. Tittle.

At the time I arrived, they were playing in Yankee Stadium. That made things in New York all the more special since it is inarguably the greatest sports stadium in the world. And the fact that the city loved the Giants, the past, and reveled in what its future might be, always made it interesting. There was a passion and hope that I have seldom seen anywhere. The city, the fans, and the franchise history added to the glitter and excitement already present in the Big Apple.

When I arrived in New York, the Giants had Earl Morrall at quarterback—but he had a horrible year in 1966, and the team had finished the season 1–12–1. Allie Sherman, the head coach of the Giants, was on the hot seat.

The Giants were in competition for fans with their crosstown rivals, the New York Jets and wildly popular quarterback, Joe Namath. It was partly the Giants' thinking that I, coming in as the new quarterback, could grab some of the attention that was being received by Namath. At one point Wellington Mara, the owner of the Giants, asked me if I would cut my hair shorter so I would have a different appearance from the Broadway Joe image. Let's just say I didn't rush off to the barbershop.

So I was brought in to New York to be the number one quarterback; Morrall went on to greatness elsewhere, with the Baltimore Colts and the Miami Dolphins. We saw immediate improvement in '67, and had a much-improved year in 1970 with nine wins. We had some pretty good players but we were not strong at several positions. Even so, there were some outstanding athletes like Tucker Frederickson, Joe Morrison, Bob Lurtsema, and Fred Dryer. I also had the opportunity to play with Homer Jones, a tremendous receiver who could really run. We worked endless hours together to form a pretty good pass-receiving duo. He and I basically ran four simple patterns: a slant to the middle of the field, an up-field sprint route, a run to the post, and a five-yard hitch pattern. That was all we needed.

There was one year when Homer caught 13 touchdown passes in the 14-game season. I loved to throw to him and he could really make a play exciting to watch after he caught the football. I also remember one year in the Pro Bowl, watching Homer outrun the great Cowboys sprinter Bob Hayes in the 100-yard dash, in full uniform. He could really fly.

The great Y.A. Tittle used to come to Giants training camp to work with us on the passing game, and he was terrific. He was the salt of the earth and I believe there was no quarterback who ever played the game better than Yelberton Abraham Tittle. And I had the incredible good fortune of being able to work with him and learn from him. He had an incredibly successful career, and

"He was an extremely smart player and I had very high regard for him both as a person and as a player. I believe he understood the passing game better than any quarterback that I ever worked with."

—ALLIE SHERMAN, FORMER HEAD COACH, NEW YORK GIANTS

so much to teach me. Many years later, after both of us had long put football aside, we hooked up as tennis partners and went down to Sea Island, Georgia, to play a match with some area tennis pros. We beat them! Y.A. loved to play tennis and he was great at it, too.

Joe Walton helped develop and mold our passing attack, similar to what is now called a West Coast offense. Ours involved motion plays and multiple formations to force the defense to adjust to our offense, which was still basically the same few plays. We built some very good offensive football in New York with Joe Walton and Y.A.

I am in love with New York City! It is like no other place anywhere in the world. It has the best of everything and is truly the greatest city on this earth, and I loved playing there. The fans were absolutely fantastic! They would boo and they would cheer but there was never any hate. They loved their players. Their passion for the game is second to none.

Even after all these years, every time I go back to New York, which I do twice a year, they remember. Policemen, firemen, taxi drivers, and fans, all greet me, "Hey, Fran!" I walk down the street and they'll give me a hip fake, like I am still scrambling. It means a lot to me, especially after all these years.

The East Coast fan mentality is unique. A young man who works for me went back home to Philadelphia this past year after their World Series victory just to enjoy the celebration after the win! Only in the northeast.

"Defensive players hated him because we could never catch him—and we chased him everywhere...."

—"BENCHWARMER" BOB LURTSEMA, FORMER NEW YORK GIANTS AND MINNESOTA VIKINGS

My time in New York was an incredible learning experience for me. For a 27-year-old to be set loose in New York...there was nothing else like it! The world revolves around New York City. You have people of every ethnicity, every type of food, Broadway plays, and something going on every day. It is the most exciting city anywhere and it was a wonderful education.

In addition to all that the city had to offer, I was the quarterback for the New York Giants, playing in "the House that Ruth Built," Yankee Stadium! The history, the mystique, everything about it was unbelievable. Yankee Stadium was, of course, a baseball place, where Ruth and Gehrig, Mantle, and DiMaggio played. Yet it is easy to forget, with all its baseball history, that the greatest game in the history of professional football was played in Yankee Stadium in 1958. Alan "the Horse" Ameche ran the ball into the end zone in overtime to defeat the Giants and crown the Baltimore Colts champions. It is often referred to as "the greatest game ever played." It was the first time in the history of the National Football League that a game had been decided by overtime play, and it was for the NFL Championship. The game helped to establish the popularity of the National Football League in today's sports market.

A clubhouse man at the stadium by the name of Pete Sheehy would tell us stories of Ruth, Gehrig, and DiMaggio. Think about it! Babe Ruth played there! It brought a chill.

One of my very favorite family pictures is of my son, Matthew, when he was about two years old. He is sitting on a tarp on the field, with a Giants hat on, watching one of our practices. This year, Matthew went to New York to see one of the final games in the old Yankee Stadium and sat right behind that tarp. It made a great picture and brought back so many wonderful memories for me.

When the Vikings sent me to the Giants, it was a big trade. In exchange for me, Minnesota obtained four draft choices. Ultimately, they were Bob Grim, Clinton Jones, Ed White, and future Hall of Famer Ron Yary. They were all contributing players who formed a foundation for the great Minnesota teams that soon followed.

But in New York, we suffered during my tenure. We didn't have enough great players. During one period, I was taller than all our offensive tackles, and although we had a formidable center in Greg Larson from Minnesota, we couldn't compete personnelwise with the upper echelon of the league. It became very frustrating for me. I wanted to win and it became apparent to me during the five years I played there that it was not going to happen in New York.

The New York Giants have had a winning tradition since its establishment in 1925. Only the Green Bay Packers and the Chicago Bears have won more championships. When I first arrived, Allie Sherman was the head coach. Allie didn't deserve the tough time he received from the New York fans; he was a class act, and he took most of the abuse pretty well. But New York fans have very little patience, and were pretty rough on him when the Giants weren't winning, which at that time was plenty.

The time that I played for the Giants was a period of transition in many respects. In the early '60s, the Giants reached the title game in three consecutive years. After that, they were hit with many injuries and retirements from key personnel. By the time the late-'60s and early-'70s came, the team was in disarray; winning consistently was not the norm.

The great Giants teams of the past stepped aside for future dynasties like the Dallas Cowboys, Pittsburgh Steelers, and the Minnesota Vikings. When the Vikings started winning on a regular basis under Bud Grant, it was extremely hard for me to take. When Joe Kapp led the Vikings to the Super Bowl against the Kansas City Chiefs in 1969, I was jealous. It was a very difficult time for me. I felt like it was my team, my friends, and something we had built together. They were going to the championship game and I was left behind.

But we did the best we could on the New York Giants. The players were also my friends and they all worked hard. We just didn't have the quality and caliber of players that some of the other championship clubs did.

Sherman was an outstanding coach to play for; I loved the man. He was absolutely the nicest person you would ever want to meet. I used to go to his home on Monday nights to have dinner with his wife and their children. Afterward, we would put together the next week's game plan. It was a wonderful working experience.

Allie Sherman really understood the game of football. He coached the Giants from 1961 to 1969, won three division titles, and was the NFL Coach of the Year twice—something most coaches since the inception of the league will never be able to claim.

Believe it or not, he once played for an NFL team called the Steagles, comprised of players from the Pittsburgh Steelers and Philadelphia Eagles and put together due to manpower shortages caused by World War II. Overall, he played in 51 NFL games before retiring and becoming a coach.

But as the losses accumulated, the fans really got on him. They used to sing this song, "Good-Bye, Allie." It was awful to hear, and I know it must have hurt him greatly but he never showed it. They never broke him, and I respect him for the way he handled it.

After a dismal loss in a preseason game at the beginning of the 1969 season, the New York fans prevailed in their wishes and Allie Sherman was fired. He was succeeded by former Giants All-Pro running back Alex Webster. It was a most interesting sequence of events that got him there.

Everyone loved Alex Webster. He played college football at North Carolina State University, and was drafted in the 11th round of the NFL Draft by the Washington Redskins in 1953. He never played for Washington, but chose instead to play in Canada with the Montreal Alouettes from 1953

"He was one of the very best of the best."

—ALLIE SHERMAN

to 1954, where he made the Canadian All-Star Team in 1954. The following year, Alex returned to the United States to play football and was with the New York Giants from 1955 to 1964. While with the Giants, he scored 56 touchdowns and was twice named to the Pro Bowl. Not bad for an 11th round draft pick. He eventually became an assistant coach under Sherman, and in 1969, after Sherman's dismissal, he was named the head coach of the New York Giants. The move came as a surprise to everyone—not least of all Alex.

Upon hearing the dismal news of the Sherman firing, Alex headed out on the town to drown his sorrows. He had been an assistant coach under Sherman but was not high enough on the chain of command to be in consideration for the head coaching position. So when he heard that Wellington Mara was looking for him, he expected the meeting to be his last official act with the club. In other words, he expected to be fired.

He arrived at the Giants' offices at 10 Columbus Circle in New York City prepared to accept his termination. The conversation went something like this:

Mara: Alex, you know we fired Allie Sherman.

Webster: Yes, I know you did.

Mara: Alex, we have thought long and hard about who should be the next head football coach of the New York Football Giants, and we have decided that it should be you.

Webster: Are you —— me?!

Not long after Webster was named the Giants' head coach, he made a call to offensive line coach and former player Roosevelt Brown, to tell him the news. Apparently *that* conversation went something like this:

"Roosevelt, this is Alex. I have just been named head coach of the New York Giants."

Roosevelt's reply was brief and to the point. "You're drunk!" he said, and then hung up.

I really enjoyed playing quarterback for Webster. He has a good soul and a big heart. And he did a pretty fair job in his role; he was named UPI's NFL Coach of the Year in 1970 when we finished second in the NFC East with a 9–5–0 record. At the helm of the Giants, from 1969 to 1973, he accumulated 29 wins, 40 losses, and one tie.

At the end of the 1971 season, I realized that I was not going to be on a championship team with the New York Giants. It seemed to me as though things were constantly in turmoil. My good friend Bob Lurtsema— probably our best defensive lineman at the time— recalls playing next to 23 different teammates during his years in New York. That could be some kind of record in itself. It was the reality of what was happening there at the time.

At the end of the season, I went to Wellington Mara and asked to be traded. Never in a million years did I expect to be traded back to the Minnesota Vikings.

It was a dream come true for me. During my absence, I had watched the Vikings grow into an NFL powerhouse. I had fought the jealousy of not leading them to that first Super Bowl. After all, it was my team! Many of the players there were close friends. And I was going back to join them.

One of my best memories with the Giants was a game we played against the Vikings. It was the 1969 season opener, and we defeated them 24–23. We had an outstanding game plan and a little tip from me. I saw "Ol Ozzie" [Dave Osborn] and "Boom Boom" [Bill Brown] line up and they tipped off what they were going to do. Because I knew them so well, I was able to use it against them. The Vikings were a tremendous football team (and they proved it with a 12-game winning streak after our game), but we had their number that day.

So I left the Big Apple with many wonderful memories and returned to the Twin Cities to play once again with a special group of players on a special team. The Vikings were now a team of seasoned veterans with impressive experience, and they had developed a habit and a passion for winning.

"I recall ...when he was with the Giants and they were playing the Vikings. Nancy Alderman and I went out to New York for the game. In the beginning, our Vikings were ahead and I actually felt sorry for Fran. And then he beat us! Then I was sorry I had felt that way for a moment."

—PHYLLIS TINGELHOFF, WIFE OF MICK TINGELHOFF

When I put the purple on for the second time in my career, I had the opportunity to be with my friends again, on and off the field. More importantly, I met the person who has had more influence on my life than any one individual I have ever known.

CHAPTER 8

Bud Grant— My Teacher, Mentor, and Coach

*Bud Grant has more common
sense than anyone I know.
I always wanted to stand next to
him at practice and in the
games because I wanted to soak
up everything he had to say.*

I'm not sure if Bud Grant knows the impact he has had on my life. It is not something you could just sit down and talk about with him.

Even so, outside of my father there is no one who has had the influence on me that he has. I can sit with friends and tell Bud Grant stories all day long. And every time I tell them, they get better! I don't mean to say that I embellish the stories the more I tell them either; I just enjoy them more and more every time I tell them.

Grant is simply the type of guy who has it figured out. He possesses a shrewd understanding of people and of the way things should be better than anyone. He is a magnificent student of people and a great manager.

I began to see how Grant worked during my first training in Mankato, Minnesota, when I returned to the Vikings. Sure, I had heard all about his idiosyncrasies, but I had not experienced them firsthand. That changed soon enough.

At the end of one of our practices, Bud gave a short talk to the team. He told us when we walk from the dormitory to the locker room there is a section of grass that some players had been walking across. The area was full of freshly planted seed, fenced off to some extent, and that we shouldn't walk on it. If we did, the grass wouldn't grow. It was a reasonable request but I remember thinking it somewhat strange at the time.

The next morning, one of our ball boys came into my room to tell me that Coach Grant wanted to see me. When I got to Bud's room, he was looking out the window. He told me to come over and look out the window with him.

"There now, do you see what I see?" he asked.

I told him I didn't. Bud continued, "Remember last night after practice when I mentioned the new grass over there being trampled on by players going to practice? Well, look, there goes one right now. There's another. Now, those players walking across the newly planted grass are not defying me. And they are not deliberately ignoring what I said last night, I understand that. Most of the players are walking around the area. But some players—look, there goes another one—they don't see the signs. They don't get it. Someday, in a game when we need them to be aware of what is going on around them, they won't be able to see what is right in front of them. They will make a critical mistake at the wrong time, and it will cost us the football game. And those players cannot play for the Minnesota Vikings."

It was clear to me what he was saying. People need to see what is right in front of them. Otherwise, how can they assess the importance of what is happening at critical moments during a football game? He knew that players like that could not play for him. I would discover that this was vintage Bud; he always had a unique way of putting things in perspective.

He has more common sense than anyone I know. I always wanted to stand next to him at practice and in the games because I wanted to soak up everything he had to say. He was the best teacher I ever had. His messages and expectations were never in doubt; though he had an unusual way of getting his point across. You had to think about it.

I recall a critical game for us at the old Met Stadium. It was a must-win, and it looked as though it could go either way as we neared the end of the fourth quarter. The Lions punted the ball and Charlie West caught it on our 5-yard line. Charlie was a smart player and a fantastic teammate but he broke a cardinal rule.

You might not find it written in any rule book, but anyone who has ever returned punts will tell you, *never catch a punt inside your own 10-yard line.* Statistically, it just doesn't make any sense to do it. There is a good chance you will get tackled immediately, whereas if you let the ball go, it will most likely travel into the end zone and your team will get a touchback and field position at the 20-yard line.

Well, Charlie broke that unwritten rule and caught the ball at the 5-yard line—and to the astonishment of everyone, returned it 95 yards for a touchdown. The place went absolutely nuts. It was bedlam at Metropolitan Stadium. We won the game and the division title, and it's all thanks to Charlie West!

I was standing on the sideline next to Bud throughout the whole thing. It was spectacular. The noise in the stadium was thunderous, but over the din I could hear Bud calmly saying, "Charlie... Charlie..." I don't know how Charlie heard him over the din, but he did, and he made his way over.

Calmly and quietly, Bud said, "Charlie, if you ever do that again, you will never play another down for the Minnesota Vikings."

The fact that he returned the ball 95 yards for a touchdown and won the game for us was immaterial. A player should never catch the ball inside the 10-yard line, period. It may have won the game for us this time, but it could cost us the game next time. That was Bud, and he was right.

In that moment, that Bud had an incredible impact on my life with those few somber words. I learned the value of discipline and it was a lesson that has enabled me to do many of the things in my life to make me successful.

Bud became the Vikings' head coach in 1967 after several successful seasons with the Winnipeg Blue Bombers of the Canadian Football League. He coached for 18 seasons and led the Vikings to 11 division championships and four Super Bowls. He has become the face of the franchise and remains legendary in the hearts of Minnesota fans.

Bud was a great athlete in his own right. He was a three-sport letterman in football, basketball, and baseball at the University of Minnesota and was a player on the great Minneapolis Lakers basketball teams of the '50s. Bud also played professional football for the Philadelphia Eagles and the Winnipeg Blue Bombers.

But his best talent by far was that he understood people and knew how to handle them. There may have been better football coaches from an X-and-O standpoint, but no one knew his players and how to teach them, reach them, and motivate them better than Bud. I have never seen him angry or heard him raise his voice. He never had to; he always got his messages across.

We used to practice at Midway Stadium in St. Paul, and I would oftentimes get there early to have coffee with some of the coaches. Some days we brought our kids in to play with each other. They would run around the stands and have a ball. I loved those days. Jerry Burns, Jocko Nelson, and other coaches would be there and we would just shoot the breeze. Bud was usually around too, and on one particular day, I had a mission. I needed to talk to him.

I figured that if anyone could give me advice, it would be Bud.

I love dogs and I have for a long time. Over the years I have had mostly German shepherds, and each one of them has brought great joy to my life. I truly believe if it weren't for dogs, there might not be much point in living. Bud is also an animal person, and I thought he could help me with my problem. I had a beautiful German shepherd named Champ, and I was having big problems housebreaking him.

I figured that if anyone could give me advice, it would be Bud. He raised dogs, trained dogs, loved dogs, and understood them. In fact, I think he had a little animal instinct in him.

I went to him and explained my problem, "Bud, you know all there is to know about dogs. I have this German shepherd. He has a pedigree and he is a great dog—but I have a problem with him. I cannot seem to find a way to housebreak the dog." I went into a detailed explanation of everything I had tried up to that point, all of the failed attempts at getting Champ to learn. I bet I went on for 15 minutes.

Through it all, Bud never altered his expression or uttered a single word. He just listened. At the end, exhausted, I said, "Bud, what should I do?"

He looked at me gravely, and without hesitation said, "Shoot him. You will do the breed a great service." It was the way his mind worked.

Grady Alderman and I used to joke about Bud all the time. We imagined that if we were stranded on a desert island, and it was the two of us against Grant for survival, Bud would eat us. We could never outsurvive him. He would have us figured out.

And what he did in managing the Vikings was give people the freedom to excel with their abilities. He knew how to manage people and he managed them in a way to allow them to succeed. He did it his way.

He has a presence about him, something few people have. When he walks in the room, you feel it. When he speaks, people listen. And they understand that he has thought it through.

*   *   *

I remember once playing the Philadelphia Eagles when Dick Vermeil was their coach. I was standing on the sideline next to Bud during the game and he turned to me and said, "Look over there at the Eagles sideline. How many coaches do you see over there?"

There we were, right in the middle of the game, and Bud had me counting coaches! I knew better than to question it. I counted 11 of them.

Bud said, "Do you know what the problem with that many coaches is? You have to figure out something for each one of them to do." These were the days when the Vikings had Bud and a handful of assistant coaches—nothing like today, when it is not unusual for teams to have as many as 20 assistants.

He managed the game better than any coach I ever played for, and he understood the risk-reward balance of every situation. I remember once coming to the sideline toward the end of a game. We had a third down and wanted to keep possession of the ball so that we could run out the clock. I wanted to know whether we should pass to try to get the first down.

Bud simply said, "I don't think if we played them for another eight quarters they could score on our defense." He didn't tell me what to do. He told me what he thought, and that was enough. That was Bud, pure and simple.

Bud wasn't into the glitz of the NFL. Cocktail parties and formal dinners were for someone else. He would rather be in the woods, watching the animals. Bud always prided himself on knowing about the weather and he was pretty good at it. He spent a great deal of time outdoors, so he had plenty of time to study it.

One day we were practicing in Mankato during training camp and I tried to "get" Bud on something. I would make every effort to try to "one up" him, but it seemed that I could never get a step ahead of him. I saw in the distance what appeared to be a violent storm approaching. I went to Bud and said, "It looks like we aren't going to get practice in today. We won't be out there ten minutes and it is going to hit us."

Bud said, "Nah, those clouds are going to go by us. What you have to worry about is when the clouds are over here." And that cloud, as if it were taking orders from Bud Grant, went right around us. Not one single drop of rain fell.

A couple weeks later, we were called in after only 20 minutes of practice. Bud announced, "You know what guys? It has been a long training camp. We have had a great 20 minutes of practice. Why don't you go in and take the rest of the practice session off. You guys have given me everything you have."

We all headed into the locker room, giddy that we'd been let loose for the day. We weren't inside more than a few seconds before it started to rain buckets.

On game days, Bud liked to get to the locker room about an hour and fifteen minutes before kickoff. For home games we would warm up about 45 minutes before the game was scheduled to start because he didn't want us sitting around in the locker room losing energy before the game. We would get taped, get dressed, and get on the field. The pregame ritual was tightly scripted by Bud. And it always worked—except for once in Detroit.

The Lions had a new stadium and we stayed in a hotel we had not stayed in before. The traffic jam on the way to the stadium was unbelievable, a huge mess. There was no chance for us to get to the stadium one hour and fifteen minutes before kickoff. After a fashion, it became apparent we weren't even going to get to the stadium before the game was to begin.

We were at a dead stop in the middle of the road. The network, the NFL, and everyone at the stadium were preparing for the game to begin and the Vikings were nowhere to be found.

I recall yelling out the window to someone, "Hey, Buddy, how far to the stadium?" And the guy says back to me, "You have no chance to get to the stadium before kickoff. You're a good 20 minutes from even getting close," and he's laughing because he doesn't know who we are. He thought we were a busload of fans trying to get to the game.

My friend and our great tight end, Stu Voigt, loves to tell this story. The bus driver at the time was horribly shaken by what was happening. As he maneuvered the bus into the parking lot at the stadium, he yelled out the window at a parking lot attendant for assistance. "I GOT THE VIKINGS! I GOT THE VIKINGS!" the driver hollered, hoping for clearance to get closer to the stadium. The parking lot attendant hollered back, " I GOT THE LIONS AND FIVE POINTS!"

I don't know exactly how late we were for the game but I think it was close to 40 minutes. Some of us were jokingly doing our warmups running the aisles of the bus. It was quite a day.

When we finally got to the locker room, everyone was in a hurry to get dressed and onto the field. Fred Zemberletti, the Vikings' trainer, was standing next to Bud. He overheard a conversation between the game's enraged referee and Coach Grant.

"The league is going to fine you for this and I am going to penalize you 15 yards on the opening kickoff for being late," he bellowed in outrage.

Bud looked calmly at him and said, "Is there anything else we can help you with today?" He then turned to his frenzied team and said, "Take your time. They can't play the game without you." That was Bud Grant.

And when the game ended we won 10–9 on a blocked kick. With all the years of losing to the Vikings, some of the Lions faithful thought the freeway problem was just a ploy by Grant to upset the Lions. Others confirmed the game was lost on the freeway. No one will ever know for sure.

Bud had some basic rules, and a lot of them were unspoken. One of them was about long hair. He used to walk by me from time to time and muss my hair a little, but he never asked me to cut it. Still, it was enough.

He had his way of doing things, which was effective. He never made any fire-and-brimstone locker room speeches. Before a playoff game against the Rams, Grant said something like this:

"Well, guys, first of all, I want to tell you it has been a great year. I want to tell you I really appreciate how you have done everything that we have asked you to do. You have been great and you are a great team. If things don't work out today, I just want to say thanks to each of you for all your support. We are playing a team today that has more talent than we do. It doesn't mean they are a better team than we are, it just means they have more talent. All of these games are tough ones and I wanted to tell you this and thank you."

That was his pep talk! His feeling was that if a coach needed to give a pep talk to get his players fired up to play in a championship game, he hadn't done his job. He relied on his players to be professionals and to know what was expected of them, as well as what they should expect from themselves.

His relationship with the media was something to watch. He really had them in his pocket. They never knew for sure what he was going to say next. He would pause a little before answering a question, just to keep them off guard.

"Fran Tarkenton is my definition of the essential quarterback... When you hear the word scrambler, it is always associated with him. In my dictionary, his picture is next to the word."

—BOB BEVARD, LONGTIME FAN

The best way to get Bud to answer your questions was never to ask his advice. Rather, you listen and you try to understand what he was saying. He didn't tell me to cut my hair. He didn't ask me not to throw the ball at the end of the Eagles game. But his observations all had meanings.

Someone recently asked me if I miss Bud Grant. I don't see him very much these days or speak to him very often. I think I surprised the person who asked by saying "no."

I don't miss Bud Grant because he is with me every day. He is a part of all that I do. He was the best football coach, the best teacher, the best manager of the game, the best manager of people, and the smartest person I have ever known.

CHAPTER 9

Greats of the Past

The real football players are the Mick Tinglehoffs and Grady Aldermans of the world. The Ellers and Marshalls, the Ray Nitschkes and Greg Larsons. These are the guys that go to the well every single play, the guys who butt heads with their opponents.

When I returned to the Minnesota Vikings in 1972, I felt blessed to rejoin a great football team. Over the next few seasons we won numerous division titles and playoff games and went to the Super Bowl three times. It was a tremendous thrill to be a part of all the winning seasons, and something I am extremely proud of.

As an NFL quarterback, I consider myself an observer. I had the opportunity to observe every aspect of the game. The fact is, quarterbacks aren't football players. We don't compete in the same way; we don't hit people and get hit on every single play.

The real football players are the Mick Tingelhoffs and Grady Aldermans of the world. The Ellers and Marshalls, the Ray Nitschkes and Greg Larsons. These are the guys who go to the well every single play, the guys who butt heads with their opponents. I have always admired them for what they do on every play, and for their willingness to put their bodies on the line.

Mick Tingelhoff, our Vikings center, was as tough as any player who ever played. If I gathered every football player that I knew or played with in my life and put them all in a room with the instructions to fight their way out, I would put my money on Mick to get there first. He was absolutely ferocious as a blocker and pass protector. He did everything. He even snapped the ball for punts, field goals, and extra points. If they kept records of how many tackles he made after interceptions and on punts, his numbers would be staggering.

Mick has been my close friend since 1962. We used to go out together and no matter where we were, I always felt I could do or say just about anything, because Mick was there to protect me, both on and off the field. He doesn't take a back seat to anybody!

On the field, when I was scrambling, Mick made some of the most devastating blocks imaginable. He took people out of plays—and sometimes out of games. He would make tough hits, clean hits that were absolutely shocking to watch. The fact that he is not enshrined in the Pro Football Hall of Fame is a major disservice to the game. He played center for 17 years and he never missed a game. He went to six Pro Bowls, four Super Bowls, and played on plenty of championship teams.

Along with Mick and Bill Brown, my other closest friend with the Vikings is Grady Alderman. He played in the trenches for the Minnesota Vikings for 14 years. Grady was as sound a football player as was ever made, a terrific offensive lineman and as steady as a rock.

We were together all the time. I remember once at the end of a season, we figured that we had said everything that could possibly ever have been said to each other, so we decided we should take a break. We didn't talk to each other for two months. We laugh about that often.

I spent a lot of time with Mick and Grady when we were on the road, and they loved ribbing me about Bart Starr. In the early days, we had a lot of trouble beating Green Bay. I recall one time when we were in Green Bay, staying at the Northland Hotel. Right across the street was a place called Chili John's. We decided to try it.

> "I used to love to tease him, call him old rag arm, and always ask him, 'Why don't you do it like Bart Starr over there in Green Bay?' He seemed like a brother to me."
>
> —MICK TINGELHOFF, FORMER CENTER, MINNESOTA VIKINGS

I get my dinner and the server asks me what kind of sauce I put on. Their hot sauces were labeled mild, hot, and extra hot. I told him, "I put on the hot sauce." He told me, "Bart Starr puts on the "extra hot." Grady looked at me and mimicked, "Bart Starr puts on the extra hot." So I went up and got the extra hot—and I was up all night.

But we beat the Packers the next day! So every time we went back to Green Bay, we went to Chili John's and I got the "extra hot," just like Bart Starr.

I feel fortunate that these guys have been in my life for so many years. The best way to describe the two of them is to simply say they just don't come any better in life than Mick Tingelhoff and Grady Alderman!

During my 18 years in the NFL I had the opportunity to meet and play with so many incredible people.

Bill Brown came to the Vikings in 1962 in a trade from the Chicago Bears and stayed in Minnesota for the next 13 years. And what a great player he was! No. 30 played the game with a sense of urgency and with an uncompromising toughness. Jerry Burns used to coach with Vince Lombardi in Green Bay, and he said that Lombardi would often assert that there were only two players in the league who had the ability to totally disrupt what the Packers had planned on any given Sunday. And one of those players was Brown.

He absolutely loved every aspect of the game. He loved every second on the field, off the field, and in the locker room. He even loved to practice! Most of all, he loved delivering that hit on people.

Bill was not only a terrific ball carrier and a crushing blocker, but he also had great hands and was as good as any receiver I've thrown the ball to. And when he had too many years under his belt to be an every-day player, he played on the special teams. His job was to barrel down the field on kickoffs and break up the wedge. Who better to do it than Bill Brown? He was a pure football player and a great teammate.

I was the quarterback for some tremendous running backs in my career. Another was Dave Osborn from the University of North Dakota. Dave was a guy who never gave up on a play. There is not a bad bone in Dave Osborn's body. He is simply a great human being. He played the game with great pride and honor.

Brown and Osborn were in our backfield together, and when Chuck Foreman arrived, we had a good thing going. Chuck could catch the ball and was a great runner—deceptive and very difficult to tackle. We always tried creative ways to get the ball to him; he was a versatile running back. Along with Brent McClanahan, these guys complemented our offense, making us a multifaceted football team.

I used to love throwing to Jim Lindsey. He was terrific at coming out of the backfield to catch the ball. He was a smart football player who had figured out the game. He prided himself on his ability to run pass patterns and was a wonderful third-down back, someone you could rely on to make the critical play.

I sure would be remiss if I didn't also mention Oscar Reed. Remember the old saying, "Give the seed to Oscar Reed"? Oscar was a good guy and fit in well with our offense. He was another hard-nosed player in a long line of extremely talented backs. It was a group of running back *par excellence*. As a quarternback, I couldn't have wished for a more talented, hardworking group.

*   *   *

In 1976, I had the opportunity to play with one of the most gifted pass receivers I have ever seen on a football field. His incredible athleticism, balance, and gracefulness were breathtaking to watch. He was truly poetry in motion. As fate would have it, he was also moments away from never playing a down for the Minnesota Vikings. His name was Ahmad Rashad.

Rashad, known when he came out of college as Bobby Moore, was a No. 1 draft choice for the St. Louis Cardinals. He went to St. Louis, then Buffalo, and wound up in Seattle after the expansion draft. He didn't get along there, so he ended up being traded to the Vikings.

We no longer had our great receiver, John Gilliam, and Sammy White was an unproven rookie. We were desperate for a receiver when Rashad showed up at practice one day.

He stepped on that field, and before long, I was like a kid in a candy store. He was coming up with everything I threw at him. He ran outs, ups, posts, hitches, quick outs, and he beat everybody on our team! I had never seen anyone like him before.

I came home that night and told my wife that I had just met the best receiver I have ever thrown the ball to in my life! We were beyond lucky to have landed him. I mean, we picked this guy up in a trade! I had been playing for 15 years in the NFL and I had never seen anyone like him. And he didn't make the Seattle Seahawks expansion team? I was elated; I told her that Ahmad Rashad was going to have a major impact on our team.

There is an unspoken mentality in football that is basically, if a player doesn't go down the field and knock someone's head loose, he can't play the game. In other words, if he doesn't play nasty, he's not a player. Guys who have the ability to flatten people are the ones who earn respect.

Ahmad was not that kind of player. He was elegant and regal. He was a sophisticated football player and had such gracefulness about him. I suspect his even-temperedness was the reason those teams let him go. They never saw how good a player he was.

I arrived at practice the next day busting at the seams. I was eager to get out there and throw to him. When I got there, Rashad was sitting in the locker room with his street clothes on. That worried me. I asked him what he was doing and he told me that the coaches asked him not to get dressed and to wait there until they returned.

It was not a good sign. Usually, when someone is told to not dress it means that the team is getting ready to release him or has just traded him. I was upset. I went to Stubby Eason, our equipment manager, to find out what was going on. He told me it was Bud who had asked Rashad not to dress.

I marched straight into Bud's office and asked him what was going on. He said that general manager Mike Lynn was concerned about Rashad's knee. He was worried we might have to pay him and then have him sit injured on the bench.

Bud asked me if I had noticed that Rashad had trouble when he had to push off on his one leg. He indicated that the Vikings had heard he had a bad knee in Seattle.

I was wound up now. I said, "I don't care if he can't push off! Did you see what he did on the field? He beat every player we had out there! He caught everything I threw at him! No one could cover him! He was better with a bad leg than anyone we had! What else does he have to do?"

Bud reiterated that Lynn was worried about a potential injury.

I told Bud that we needed to get Lynn on the phone. That is how I do business. I always want to get things moving and settled as quickly as possible.

I had paid my dues, played 15 years in the NFL, and I needed to say my piece. Ahmad Rashad was too good a football player for us to lose. So we got Lynn on the phone, and I told him to get Seattle on the phone to work out a contractual arrangement because we had to have this kid.

I said, "Mike, if Ahmad Rashad is not dressing for practice today, then *I'm* not dressing for practice!"

Rashad turned out to be a wonderful player for the Minnesota Vikings.

I truly believe that you need to fight for the things you feel strongly about. I believed in Ahmad and I was able to convince Lynn and keep him in Minnesota.

Ahmad and I went to the Pro Bowl together, and Roger Staubach, who was also there, told me that he was absolutely amazed at what

Rashad was capable of doing on the field and that he was magnificent in every respect. Roger was right, of course, and the proof was in Ahmad's incredible career.

Sammy White was the other receiver in camp that year, and he was spectacular. I loved working with Sammy. He was able to make cuts on the football field like I had never seen before, and he had natural speed. When he was in college at Grambling, he broke some longstanding track and field records that the great Jesse Owens had set. Burnsie used to tease Sammy all the time, saying things like, "Yeah, some record. Jesse Owens is 75 years old!"

I love Ahmad and Sammy as players, but mostly because they are exceptional people.

I loved Ahmad and Sammy as players but mostly because they are exceptional people. They were without question the best wide receivers I threw to in my career.

I met Bob Lurtsema, better known as "Lurtsey" or "Benchwarmer" Bob, when I came to the Giants. He was our best defensive lineman in New York. He had a great sense of humor and was so much fun to be around. New York should never have let him go.

He was the player representative for the Giants and Wellington Mara, the Giants owner, asked him for a favor. Mara had always wanted to be a friend of the players and hung around the team in an attempt to form good relationships. He asked Bob to find out what the players thought of him. He took his assignment very seriously and went to each and every guy on the team. After completing the assignment, he went back to Mr. Mara.

"You have no rapport with the team," he said, giving an honest and true assessment of what the players had told him. Three hours later, the Giants put Bob Lurtsema on waivers. Never mind that he was the best defensive player on the team.

When Lurtsey came to the Vikings in 1971, his playing time had diminished considerably. He was playing behind the famous Purple People Eaters: Jim Marshall, Carl Eller, Alan Page, and Gary Larsen. Lurtsema made hay out of his status by becoming a pitchman for Twin City Federal Savings and Loan in which he played "the old benchwarmer." Those commercials ran for years. And when the Vikings traded him to Seattle, he made a commercial that showed him loading his bench on top of an old Ford Falcon on his way to the West Coast.

> *"Fran always listened to his teammates, had earned great respect from players, and had a wonderful sense of humor."*
>
> —"BENCHWARMER" BOB LURTSEMA, FORMER NEW YORK GIANTS AND MINNESOTA VIKINGS DEFENSIVE LINEMAN

Another ad featured being honored at the old Met Stadium on "Bob Lurtsema Day," and the stands were completely empty. Those commercials were television classics. And Bob is a classic, and a terrific friend.

One of my favorite players from my time with the Giants was tight end Bob Tucker. He was a blocking tight end who had great hands. Early in his career with the Giants, he was low on the depth chart and in danger of being cut. Our defense told me that Bob was one of the toughest and best blockers on the team. Once I found that out, I made sure he got some extra looks from me and got the ball to him as much as I could so that the coaches could see his talent. Later on, I lobbied the Vikings to get him there.

When Carl Eller came to Vikings in 1964, he was recognized immediately as an incredible talent. There were few things Carl couldn't do on the football field. Jim Lindsey once said of him, "He is the greatest physical specimen I have ever seen. It was as if he had been chiseled out of stone."

During my first tour with the Vikings, Carl was still young and did some things during games that were hard to fathom. I saw him

literally throw people aside as if they were mannequins. He was magnificent in every aspect of how he played the game. He is a Hall of
Fame player and one of the best to ever play the game. He also has
great presence, an aura about him. Whatever it was, Eller had it and
he was special.

One of the aspects of professional football that is frequently over-
looked is one that often decides the outcome of a game. This, of
course, rests on the shoulders—
and the foot—of a team's kicker.
If I had one field goal or one
extra point that I had to have
made, I would want Cox kicking
it. Most Vikings fans don't know
that Fred Cox is the franchise's
all-time leading scorer. Over his
career he scored 1,365 points.
Fred was also a great athlete who
played running back at the
University of Pittsburgh.

*"I do have one sack against
Fran Tarkenton. I had him in
my sights and was zeroing in
on him, when all of a sudden
he slipped and fell down. I
went up to him, touched him,
and said, 'gotcha!'"*

—"BENCHWARMER" BOB LURTSEMA

Fred could hold a conversa-
tion about anything. And he wasn't shy about stating his opinion.
Most often, he was right. He was very, very smart and was a font of
information.

Fred and I used to ride together to practice. And when we didn't,
we would drive to practice separately and talk to each other for miles
on our CB radios.

Fred could talk a blue streak, and he was exactly the same person
talking on the sideline, in the locker room, or at a restaurant as he was
in the games in the heat of battle. I honestly don't think the man ever
felt any pressure when he was called upon to do his job. It didn't
matter if we were ahead in the game, behind, or if the kick would

decide the game's outcome—he was always steady. After the kick, if he missed it or made it, his demeanor was unchanged. He had the perfect disposition for a kicker. And he was a solid kicker for us for 15 years.

If Tommy Mason could have stayed healthy, I think he would have gone down in history as one of the very best running backs to have ever played the game. He was tremendous. He could run the football like few players I had ever seen. He was the Vikings' number-one draft choice in 1961 coming out of Tulane. He was a smart player and had a wonderful attitude—he just couldn't stay healthy. When we were all young and playing for the Vikings, Bill Brown, Tommy, and I were called "10, 20, 30," after our jersey numbers. (I know, I know, I should have been number 62, but as long as Jack Scarbath is OK with it, I am too! Besides, 62, 20, 30 doesn't have that ring to it.)

In the early '60s with old Bill "Boom Boom" Brown and Tommy Mason in the backfield and the two of them running, blocking, and receiving the ball, we were something to be reckoned with. Mason was a guile runner, a great teammate, and a fine person.

And then, there was the King. They called him the King because he was the best, maybe one of the best ever! Hugh McElhenny didn't belong in Minnesota in 1961, joining a team of cast-offs from other clubs, rookies, and aging veterans. He was too good a player, and had too much legacy to essentially start all over with a new club, new faces, and little chance to win.

When he arrived in camp, we were all in awe of him. His grace and poetic ability to run the football seemed out of place compared to everyone else. We wanted autographs! His running was nothing short of beautiful. That's not easy to say about football, but that was Hugh McElhenny.

He was really something. He had a Cadillac, he was a sharp dresser, and he had a magnificent charm. And still with all that, he came to an expansion team and became just another one of the guys. The great Hugh McElhenny, one of the guys!

Before one of Hugh's last games with us in Chicago, he was presented with a plaque from some writers that said, "Wouldn't it be wonderful if everyone played the game with the love and passion of Hugh McElhenny?" It was true. It would have been wonderful.

I can honestly say that I have never seen a better running back at any time in my career or after. I saw him return a punt 50 yards for a touchdown against his old team, the 49ers, and nine opposing players got a hand on him but none could take him down. He had the ability to do things on the football field that I have never seen anyone do. He was the real deal, an incredible player.

*   *   *

Aside from the players, another person who was incredibly special was our trainer, Fred Zamberletti. I loved to get my ankles taped by Fred because it meant listening to him talk—and he didn't have to say a word because he talked more with his hands than anyone I ever knew! No one in the world ever said a bad thing about him.

He has left an indelible impression on the Minnesota Vikings. He was there in the beginning and he is still there! He's the eyes and the ears of the place. He knows more about the team, the coaches, and life in general than anyone else. He is intuitive, funny, insightful, and extremely bright. He always gets the big picture.

Fred, along with longtime equipment manger, Stubby Eason, formed the fabric and foundation for what the Vikings were to become. This franchise would not have seen its success without them. They were with us on the field, in the locker room, and by our side when we needed them. They made the whole thing all worthwhile!

Jerry Reichow has been with the organization almost five decades as a player and personnel man. He might have been our best player during our inaugural season in 1961. He was instrumental in teaching me professional football along with another teammate, Dr. Dave Middleton. It bears repeating that the two of them were tremendous football players. These two guys together saved my bacon because they took me under their wing and taught me NFL defenses, as well as about other teams' personnel. They were great teachers and leaders.

I also loved to throw the ball to Stu Voigt, our tight end. He was a three-sport letterman at Wisconsin in track, baseball, and football. He was a very smart and disciplined player, a dependable tight end for the Vikings for 11 years. Stu was one of my roommates for a while, and he was always fun to be around. I'd bet that there is no one who enjoyed putting on a Viking uniform more than he did; he was always proud to wear the purple colors.

In addition to the fine teammates I had over the years, I also tip my hat to some of the formidable competitors I played against. The best defensive football player that I have ever seen play the game or have known, undoubtedly, was the great Baltimore Colt defensive end, Gino Marchetti.

> *"Fran Tarkenton would do absolutely everything he could do to win a football game."*
>
> —STU VOIGT, FORMER TIGHT END, MINNESOTA VIKINGS

I played in the Pro Bowl with him. The Cleveland Browns had recently beaten the Colts in the NFL Championship game. The Browns were way ahead, nearing the end of the game and Frank Ryan, the Cleveland quarterback, called a timeout to try to score again. A bunch of players at the hotel in Hawaii were talking about it and how unprofessional it was to run up the score. I was sitting near Gino—I wanted to hear everything he said because I thought he was such a great player. As the conversation went on, I heard Gino say quietly to himself, "I'm going to get him."

On the third or fourth play of the game, Gino busts through the line and as Frank Ryan is going back to pass, grabs him, picks him up, throws him to the ground, and breaks his shoulder. Terry Barr, who I was sitting next to on the sidelines, looked over at me and said, "Well, Gino is the only one I know who can say he is going to get someone, and he does!" Terry heard him say it too.

When I was with the Giants, I once saw Gino destroy one of our big tackles. The rookie tackle had put Vaseline all over his jersey so Gino couldn't get ahold of him. I dropped back to pass and I heard this awful noise behind me. He tore our guy's jersey right off his back! And then yelled at him to get a new jersey and "keep that —— off of it." That was Gino. He was a man among men and the greatest defensive end I have ever seen play the game.

Bob Lilly from Dallas was also exceptional and so was Merlin Olsen from the Rams. "Mean" Joe Greene from the Steelers is in the same category; he was a tremendous force on the defensive side of the ball. I think that Alan Page, in his prime, was certainly as good as the rest of them. He could literally take over a football game with his ability. I think Bill George was as good as his Bears predecessor, Dick Butkus. Ray Nitschke of the Packers was a terrific linebacker, too. And Chuck Bednarik of the Eagles was an absolute monster. He was one of the last players to play both ways, as center on offense and middle linebacker on defense.

I get asked to rate quarterbacks frequently, and many people are surprised by my answer. My top three would be Otto Graham, Y.A. Tittle, and Roger Staubach. All three of them had it all. They were smart players, stalwart leaders who really understood the game and were terrific in the clutch. And they played superior football throughout their long careers.

Of the three of them, I think Tittle was the best. I truly respect him. I was fortunate to have known him well. I'll never forget the photograph of him on his knees during a game in the heat of battle, worn and dirty, with blood running down his face. Tittle had "the face", the heart, and the skills. Y.A. Tittle had all the right stuff.

Graham was also a terrific player. He had a real presence about him and could always get the job done.

And Staubach, even though he threw the Hail Mary against us, still goes down as one of the best on my list. Roger has "the face," the character, the humility, and the drive. He made the plays over and over for the Dallas Cowboys, and has also been a real success in life.

Someone once asked me where I was on the list; in other words, where did I rate myself as a quarterback compared to Tittle, Graham, Staubach, and all the rest. I answered him this way, "If I were going to pick one quarterback to take the field to win one game, I would pick Fran Tarkenton." What can I say? I would want to be the one with the game on the line to have it all rest on my shoulders. I think a lot of competitors feel that way. The drive to succeed is in our blood.

CHAPTER 10

When the Cheering Stopped

I loved the Twin Cities and New York City, but my roots were in the South. I needed to go home and I wanted to separate myself from being Fran Tarkenton, quarterback of the Minnesota Vikings.

After 18 years in the National Football League from 1961 to 1978, it was over.

I took a knee, allowing the clock to run out against the Los Angeles Rams at the end of the 1978 season. It was a loss in the 1978 playoffs and the last game of my career. Football had been a major part of my life since I was a boy. It was now done.

Looking back on it now, I would have done some things differently, but I am satisfied by what I accomplished. I wish Norm Van Brocklin and I could have worked together longer because we would have won a lot of games. I certainly would have gone along with Jerry Burns' recommendation to run the ball on that late-game third-down play against Dallas in 1975. There are other things and other games that I would execute differently if I had the chance, but it doesn't work that way. It's just like a career in any other profession. You wish that you knew as much the first day on the job as the last day because you could have been so much better at it.

After that season ended in Los Angeles, I decided to return to Georgia permanently. I loved the Twin Cities and New York City, but my roots were in the South. I needed to go home and I wanted to separate myself from being Fran Tarkenton, quarterback of the Minnesota Vikings.

I made $12,500 my first year playing professionally for the Vikings in 1961, and I was the highest paid professional football player when I retired. But I wanted to move on and be successful at something else, and even more importantly, put my roots down.

I believe that I could not have grown personally or professionally had I stayed in the Twin Cities. I would always be Fran Tarkenton, the football player. I was proud of what I achieved there; I always appreciated the recognition from fans and the signing of autographs (well, most of the time anyway), but it was time to move on.

So I decided to go. And like my earlier decision to part with Van Brocklin, there was no looking back.

At first, I didn't know how much I needed to get away from the environment where I had spent so many years until I actually made the permanent move. It is nice to be recognized, but sometimes people expected too much. It was starting to take its toll on me. Most people are nice and sensitive to others' privacy, though some are not. I recall one fan whose behavior had a significant effect on me.

I had gone with my family and friends for dinner after a game. A man approached our table with his son, who I'd guess was 10 years old. The father told me that I had really let his son down by losing the game, and asked me how I could do something like that to his boy, who loved the Vikings and worshiped me. I was stunned. It was pretty sad and outrageous behavior on the part of the man and it bothered me tremendously.

I didn't go out in public much after that incident. And I knew when I took that knee the last game of my career, it was time. The spotlight and the cheering had been a wonderful part of my life for almost three decades, but the end had arrived.

To this day, it is hard for me to go back to the Twin Cities. I loved every minute of my life there, and I loved being an NFL quarterback for 18 years. It was a part of me and everything I did. But it is hard for me to retrace old territory. I have moved on and I am happy in my skin and I love my life.

I played for the Vikings for 13 years and retired there, but I do not go back to Minnesota very often to be a part of the Vikings organization or to be one of the guys. I get criticized for that. Some think it's arrogance but I sincerely do not mean it that way; I just need to do things my way. My home is here in Atlanta, and it is hard for me to go back. It takes nothing away from how I feel about the Twin Cities, the state of Minnesota, the region, the fans, or any of my teammates. It was truly a love affair for me, and something I will always cherish. I care deeply about Minnesota and the fans there who supported me and I will carry those memories with me always.

I love my friends and I have wonderful memories of the past, but I am not absorbed in it. My life has evolved and I'm tackling new challenges every day. In many ways, my business life is the same. I feel like I take the field every day and want to win.

I am 69 years old and still going full speed ahead. Studs Terkel once wrote, "I took a vacation once—it involved the beach—and to tell you the truth I had no idea what to do with myself. It was torture. Work is life. Without it, there is no life." He could have been describing my life and me. I need to be engaged in something every day. I am grateful to wake up every day with a burning desire to face the challenges that await me. And solving the problems of the day is truly the best part of it.

It is the same for me now, perhaps moreso as I meet the challenges with more experience and better solutions. Trying to figure out how to beat a blitz package of the Green Bay Packers or putting together a business deal or solution, are one in the same.

If at the end of the day my colleagues, partners, friends, family, or employees are better off for it, then we have won the game. And the victory means just as much to me today as beating the Chicago Bears did in the Vikings' inaugural 1961 game.

You see, I'm not sure the cheering ever really stops if you don't want it to. I think every day the game is on, and if you keep at it you will have the ability to make an impact.

My life after football has been concentrated on business, but I did involve myself in a few television ventures with *Monday Night Football* and *That's Incredible!*. I was also involved in some television programs with NBC. I did a program called *Grandstand*, and dabbled with some golf programs as well as some NFL football work. Then

Roone Arledge from ABC Sports contacted me about doing *Monday Night Football.*

Monday Night Football began its television run in 1970, and has been one of the longest running prime-time television programs in history. I did it for four years. I didn't like it.

Even though I worked with some incredibly interesting people, it just wasn't for me. I was not built to sit in a booth and comment on what other people are doing. It isn't a way to enjoy myself or challenge myself. *That was a great catch* or *He sure ran hard on that play*—and if one of my partners in the booth said it first, I didn't even get to say that! It certainly wasn't the same as calling the play on the 8-yard line with three seconds left, and trailing the Chicago Bears by six points.

Even so, I really enjoyed working with Frank Gifford, Don Meredith, and Howard Cosell. Gifford was very knowledgeable, a gifted broadcaster, and a true professional. He was also a great player for the New York Giants who played on both offense and defense and went to eight Pro Bowls at three different positions, which gives an indication of what an incredible football player Frank was. He was just as gifted in the booth.

Cosell had a perfect voice for the airwaves and was extremely intelligent. I really enjoyed him. He was incredibly bright, talented, and a true "character."

He used to do a live five-minute radio program, and I was often with him when he did it. It was amazing to watch. Howard never prepared for the broadcast. He would go on the air live and rattle off the current sports news, give his commentary, and then at the precise moment at the close of the five-minute program, say, "This is Howard Cosell…" and then bang! The five minutes were up. He had a gift for it. He also did the *Monday Night Football* halftime highlights with no notes and he was superb at it. He had an uncanny ability to relate to his audience.

I thoroughly loved being around Howard, though he was a very different sort of person. He craved attention; he was starved for it and would accept it from anyone. After games, he would often stay in the hotel bar for hours talking to people. He could spend the entire night talking, drinking, and smoking cigars. That was Howard.

I think I used to spend a lot of time with him because not many others would. There wasn't a close relationship between Howard and the other *MNF* guys.

Turn out the lights! The party's over! All good things must come to an end.

Don Meredith was a fabulous entertainer! He was really something. Fans around the country anxiously awaited hearing his famous game-ending chant, "Turn out the lights! The party's over! All good things must come to an end!" He has a charming personality and was a wonderful Hollywood actor. He had so many good roles, and was so remarkable in character. And of course, out of character as well. More than anything, it was just the "character" in him that makes him so special.

People sometimes forget that Don was a great football player. He was a starting quarterback for three seasons, led the Southwest Conference in completion percentage all three years, and was an All-American twice. After serving as a backup quarterback on the Dallas Cowboys for several years, he led the team to the NFL playoffs several years in a row.

I recall one game when I was working with Don and Frank. We spent most of the day out by the hotel pool and I became very sick. I had developed elephantiasis, which can be a very serious illness. It is often caused by a microscopic, threadlike parasitic worm that is transmitted by mosquitoes. It causes obstruction in the lymphatic vessels and swelling in the legs and genitals.

113

One of the team trainers diagnosed me, and he said I needed to be hospitalized immediately and be treated because it could be very serious. I was about to go on air on *Monday Night Football*; going to the hospital was out of the question. We agreed on a compromise. I would do the game, but would have to spend the entire evening icing my testicles. It could work, however uncomfortably, because I would be sitting on a stool and the camera would only show me from the waist up.

So there I was, just minutes before we were to go on live television, sitting on a stool in the booth with a yellow blazer, no pants, and an ice bag on my lap.

Meredith walked in the booth, took one look at me sitting there in my delicate position, and said, "Pardner, what are friends for," and took his pants off. He and I did the entire game without pants on. "Dandy Don" is a classic. I love him to death.

Overall, I had fun with the guys, but it didn't work for me. I enjoyed Howard, no question about that and I really enjoyed being around Frank and Don. All three were very smart men. They knew how to perform, were exceptional behind the microphone, and truly knew their audiences. I learned a great deal from all of them, and it was a pleasure to be around them.

So I left after four years, and tried some other things, including the television program *That's Incredible!*, a show set in the tradition of *Ripley's Believe It or Not.* It featured people who came on and performed some truly "incredible" stunts. It was fun, but there I was stuck again telling audiences what I was observing.

In life, as in business, I pride myself on the fact that I put myself in a position to learn from other people, as well as help others to solve problems. I am proud of the fact that I can honestly say that I have never had a completely original thought; I take everything I can learn from others. I am a sponge and soak up every ounce of knowledge and expertise that I can get, every day of my life. It is why I always stood next to Bud Grant on the sideline. I didn't want to miss anything he said. He was so smart and he taught me so much. He taught me discipline ("remember, Charlie...") and awareness.

It is extremely important for me to be around positive, knowledgeable people. People like Sam Walton, the Wal-Mart founder. He was a brilliant man and an exceptional businessman. I loved him and learned a huge amount from him.

One of my prized possessions is a letter from him. It is right up there with anything that I ever achieved on the football field, and is a further report card for me to evaluate whether life is working for me.

It reads:

Dear Fran:

I apologize for this delayed thank you note, but I want you to know how much all of us in our Wal-Mart Company and Sams' Division appreciated your visit to our grand opening of the 100th Sam's Store in Joliet, Illinois. That was quite an event and one that was made even more special by your presence and your involvement. You are some kind of rare talent.

I had the opportunity to review one of your management articles recently. Last Monday morning, we had 150 district managers in from all our Wal-Mart territories. I quoted from your article and from this particular management treatise in depth. In fact, I had copies made and sent home with all our district managers so it could be on their minds and they could have a better understanding of your philosophy. I think it parallels exactly what we should be doing within our company.

Anyway, my friend, we have the greatest respect for your leadership and the direction you are giving businesses and management all over these United States. Keep up the good work!

Thanks, too, for that football. It is on the mantle as a trophy and my grandchildren appreciate it, as well.

Take care of yourself. Come see us when you can. Best wishes for your continued success and health.

Your friend,

Sam Walton

This letter, coming from Sam Walton, is incredibly special to me. *He* is special to me. It reminds me that I am on the right path, continuing to strive in a way that meets my needs as well as those of others. My business ventures are wide-ranging, but they have all been very successful. I have started 15 companies and am looking every day for something new. I believe in challenges and opportunities and try to take advantage of them.

But my true joy in the business world and in my personal life comes from relationships. Brad Carr is an example of a cherished relationship, and the story that he told me on December 1, 2008, changed my life forever. But it is his story, so I'll let him tell it to you in his own words.

My parents divorced when I was just a few months old. I never met my father, and before I started school, my mother had our name legally changed for reasons known only to her. I've never troubled her to ask why, but I grew up always wondering where I came from.

In my midthirties, with the help of the burgeoning Internet, I did some halfhearted searching for my father and found an address in Atlanta. I didn't know whether it was him or if it was still current, and between work and family, there never seemed to be enough time or motivation to dig any deeper. But still I wondered. Finally, my amateur sleuthing revealed that my father had passed away in 1993. There the trail went cold.

Years passed, and I decided to make one last attempt to see if there were any living family members. On March 3, 2005, I left the following post on the genealogy.com website:

> "Hi,
>
> I'm a newbie, but I thought I'd give this a try. Eniobel Carrasquillo is my father. He died in 1993 and is buried in the National Cemetery in Puerto Rico. Unfortunately, I have never met him. Just wondering if he has any family over here. I'd just like to connect. I want nothing in return.
>
> Thanks for your help.
>
> Brad Carr"

There was no response. As far as I was concerned, this time the issue was closed for good.

Then, on October 19, 2008, nearly four years later, I received a short email from Rose, who claimed to be my second cousin, and who had been researching the genealogy of my father's family for the past four years. She asked me to respond to her email message if I was still interested. I learned from her that I have two aunts still living in Florida, along with a half brother living in Brunswick, Georgia, and a half sister in Miami, as well as another half sister from a third marriage, living in the Atlanta area. Just imagine, I was 50 years old, an only child, and I suddenly discovered that I had three siblings! It was extraordinary.

Rose put me in contact with my aunt Mitzi, my father's sister, and she began to tell me about her family's background.

She also gave me contact information for my three half siblings. I got on the phone right away and called all three, but wasn't able to connect with the youngest sister living in Atlanta. But my two other long-lost siblings welcomed me with open arms. I was living in southern California, but we vowed to meet face-to-face as soon as we could.

I had no idea how soon it would be.

I had a Monday-morning business meeting scheduled in Atlanta with Fran Tarkenton, and I decided to fly in the Friday before so I would have time to drive to Brunswick and meet my brother. I didn't even call to check if he was going to be there; I figured if it were meant to be, it would all work out. And if he wasn't around, I could always fly to Pensacola, Florida and spend the weekend with my mother. I also called my half sister in Miami in the off chance that she would be able to get away on such short notice. She said she would drop everything to be there.

I arrived at my half brother's home to a tearful welcome. I had to get used to being called Uncle Brad by his four children; an easy adjustment, for sure! We hugged and kissed and laughed and cried and talked until the wee hours. Then, I got to take a long walk along the beach with my half sister. She opened up about my father and their relationship. She said they knew about me and had searched for years without success. I felt we made a deep connection. I also bonded with my half brother; we talked about our dreams and aspirations. It is amazing to me how similar we are in so many ways!

On Monday morning I arrived at Fran Tarkenton's office in Atlanta. His unsuspecting receptionist made the mistake of asking how my weekend went. Being thoroughly uplifted by the weekend's events, I told her what had happened. She began to choke up and suddenly exclaimed, "Fran, you must hear this story!" And with that, I was introduced to Fran Tarkenton. He was bigger than I imagined him, but his stature paled in comparison to the size of his enormous heart, as I would soon discover.

I told him the whole story. By the end, he was grinning and shaking his head in amazement. Then I told him that the craziest part was that there's still another sister in Atlanta, but I hadn't been able to connect with her.

Right then, Fran said, "You are going to meet your sister tonight—you have my word on it. I am going to make that happen for you!" With that, Fran marshaled his troops and gave directions. His calm determination made me feel as if I was in the huddle on third-and-long, listening as he diagrammed a trick play to take advantage of an opponent's newly discovered weakness. It was as if he was telling his receivers to go long, his running back to swing out into the flats, and saying, "I'll do some scrambling till one of you breaks free. Let's get this touchdown!" Honestly, I've never experienced anything like it.

A few hours later, I was summoned to Fran's office where he filled me in. We've found your sister. I've talked to her, and she's a delightful person—you're going to just love her. And she's dying to meet you, too! I sensed some hesitation on her part and thought maybe I could help make things a little easier. So, I've hired a driver to pick up your sister and her husband and son. Then, they'll pick you up at your hotel and take you to my favorite restaurant in Atlanta."

As I started to thank him for making the arrangements, Fran cut me off. He then said to me, "And it would bless me if you would be my guest this evening."

Apparently, my half sister isn't much of a football fan— she'd never heard of Fran Tarkenton. When Jill, Fran's receptionist, put through the call, my half sister thought that he was some kind of lawyer. Quite the contrary. He explained that he had met a business associate that may be her long-lost brother. She burst into tears. You might hear it said that quarterbacks don't cry, but this one did. Fran motioned for Jill to take over the call and switch it to speakerphone. The other people in the room were in tears too.

The short ride to the restaurant was joyful as my sister and I met for the very first time. After we had settled into the restaurant, Fran and his wife Linda surprised us by stopping by our table to introduce themselves. Seeing that we had yet to order, he whispered some instructions to the waiter, who jumped into action, returning with an amazing array of food. Fran made his personal recommendations from the menu, hugged my new family members, and said good night.

The next day, as I recounted the evening to Fran, I told him he had changed my life forever. He humbly said, "Well, you've changed me forever." I believe him, and so does my younger sister, who is now Fran Tarkenton's biggest fan.

But the story isn't quite over yet. At the end of our conversation, Fran said, "Let's do lunch;" he wanted to meet the rest of the family, too. Insincere phrases like, "Let's do lunch," have never entered Fran Tarkenton's lexicon—he meant it.

From what I experienced, spending time with Fran Tarkenton is an event not to be missed. He will inspire, motivate, and captivate you. Later, when I told my siblings that Fran would like to meet them, they dropped everything to be there. They wanted to meet him not because of his celebrity, but to thank him for blessing my life and helping me to reach out to them and find them and bond with them, blessing their own lives as well.

When the Cheering Stopped

Fran, in his own disarming way, embraced each member of my family as his own. I marveled at how, during the course of our lunch, Fran asked the most detailed questions of each family member.

"What went through your mind the exact moment you spoke to your brother for the very first time?"

"I was at the reunion luncheon … [It] was an example of his effort and caring. It shows where Fran Tarkenton's heart is. He wants to make a difference in people's lives."

—Dave Reindel,
BUSINESS ASSOCIATE AND FRIEND

"Tell me specifically what you felt the very first time you saw your brother."

"What did you think when your son told you he had found his siblings, his father's family?"

Each response was thoroughly absorbed and considered, then followed with even more thoughtful, probing queries. It was obvious how sincere his interest was. He wanted to know about my siblings' lives—what they did for a living, their aspirations. He even wanted to know their expectations of a life moving forward with a new brother in it.

If asked for a single word to describe Fran, I would say genuine. He is the real deal in everything he does. I have witnessed it firsthand. Lunch was filled with laughter and very few moments were tear-free.

Why would a man like Fran Tarkenton take the time to help an average Joe like me? He didn't do it for financial gain. He didn't do it because he needed another friend. He didn't do it because he wanted another fan. He did it because he cares. He wants to give back. He wants to share. Fran wants to make the lives of those around him better.

121

Back in California, my wife and I discussed the importance of family. I told her I didn't want a once-a-year relationship with my new siblings in which we would fly down to spend a few days with them each year. I want to see them on weekends, holidays, birthdays, and anniversaries...I have 50 years of lost time to make up for. My wife and I are in the very early stages of relocating to the Atlanta area to be close to my brothers and sisters. And it doesn't hurt that Fran is there, too!

He may never fully comprehend the impact he has had on my life. He entered it when I was at an all-time low on many levels. He believed in me professionally when no one else did. He went out of his way to help me build bonds with a family I did not know. He imparts wisdom and guidance without passing judgment. And he inspires me to be an example to others. In many ways Fran, through his act of kindness, has vicariously taken the place of a deceased and absent father to bring together children separated by miles, different marriages, and the unknown. I will be forever thankful to have met Fran Tarkenton. My life will never be the same.

What happened in my offices on December 1, 2008, is more important to me than any football victory I've ever experienced. During my time with Brad and his family I learned some things about myself, too. It is an experience that has meant so much to me. I really care about other people. I really do deeply care. And when Brad told me his story, I reacted to it. We never did talk any business that day.

CHAPTER II

People I Have Met Along the Way

One of my greatest thrills in life was when my son Matthew and I met the legendary Bronko Nagurski, thought by some to be the greatest football player that ever lived.

Because of my success as a quarterback in the National Football League, and through my post-football experiences in television and other ventures, I have had the opportunity to meet many interesting people in my life. I feel very fortunate to have crossed their paths and have been blessed with an abundance of wonderful friendships. Each is different and has brought something to my life.

Johnny Carson filled up America's living rooms with his late-night show for so many years, and was a magnificent entertainer and a fan favorite. I got to know him very well and we became good friends. He was different than what most people might expect. He was quiet, unassuming, and wanted absolutely none of the Hollywood glitz. He was reserved offscreen, a far cry from his many colorful television characters.

Henry Winkler was similarly quiet and very kind. He will always be "the Fonz," but offscreen he is just a regular guy.

Another absolutely incredible person that I got to know was Lucille Ball. She was something! Just an unbelievable woman. She had a quality about her, a sort of naturalness and accessibility, that made you feel like you had known her forever. She was able to translate that onto the screen, which made her so successful. Carson and Winkler didn't want to crack wise and be the center of attention—but Lucille Ball did, and she was!

When people remember the great Yankee, Joe DiMaggio, they think of him as larger than life, as he was on the field. In reality, he was painfully shy, quiet, and uncomfortable around people. And yet, the superstar label will always fit him. I am convinced that his record of hitting safely in 56 consecutive games will never be broken.

One of my favorite superstar athletes was always the great slugger Hank Aaron of the Milwaukee—and later, Atlanta—Braves. Aaron was a special player and is a special human being. I was fortunate to meet him when the Vikings played a game against the Green Bay

Packers. He visted the training room and we met before the game. Some years later, he and I worked together on a political campaign for a mutual friend of ours. One evening, we were each scheduled to speak and I was introducing Aaron. I enumerated all his records and accolades, and then said, "but what you probably *don't* know about Hank Aaron is that he struck out more than anyone else." He laughed, and when he got up to speak he mentioned me throwing more interceptions than anyone else. We had a lot of fun with it.

Stu used to love to tell the story, "In walks Reggie Jackson. And then the next thing I know, the phone rings and it's President Ford on the line—and he doesn't want to talk to me!"

Hank Aaron is a class act, quiet, and humble. He played Major League Baseball not too long after Jackie Robinson. It is impossible to understand what those two and many others went through. The fact that he thrived during those most difficult times for him and other athletes of color speaks volumes about his character.

Some years back, I was staying at the Waldorf-Astoria Hotel in New York City. I had just finished reading the most incredible book that I had ever read; it was about General Douglas MacArthur. In it, he spoke about his wife and what a remarkable woman she was. I got on the elevator in the hotel, and Mrs. MacArthur got on with me. It was unbelievable! She was quite the lady, and I was grateful to have met her and I expressed my admiration for her husband and for her. It also brought me back to my youth, when the great General paid the city a visit. Mrs. MacArthur and I had many conversations after that chance meeting, and I sent a signed helmet to her for a museum that she was involved with in Norfolk, Virginia. I will always remember her.

When I think about the really nice people in my life, President Gerald Ford is at the top of the list. I recall once, on a road trip when

I was with the Vikings, I was rooming with my good friend, Stu Voigt. Reggie Jackson was there and we were talking when President Ford called on the phone.

Stu used to love to tell the story, "Here I am sitting in my room with Fran and the door opens and in walks Reggie Jackson. And then the next thing I know, the phone rings and it's President Ford on the line! And he doesn't want to talk to me."

President Ford had played football at the University of Michigan. He had no huge ego; he was a lovely, down-to-earth plainspoken man.

* * *

One of the real "characters" of all time was a stellar football player and a tremendous actor named Fred Dryer. He was a great college football player at San Diego State University and a first-round draft pick of the New York Giants in 1969. He played for three seasons before being traded to the Los Angeles Rams, where he played for another decade. He is as well known for his brilliant acting career. He played the lead role on *Hunter,* a television show about the LAPD homicide detectives that was extremely popular during its run from 1984 to 1991. He has numerous other acting credits and he nearly landed the role of Sam on *Cheers.*

He was also as funny as a person could be. He used to do Wellington Mara impressions that had the guys rolling. He was always doing something crazy. One year, he showed up for the last game of the season wearing multicolored bowling shoes with cleats on the bottom—and wore them through the whole game. He was unbelievable!

When Fred was a rookie, he lived in a Volkswagen bus. Some years later on Christmas Eve, he called our house and asked me if he could stop over. He stayed two weeks.

I met Don Engel in New York City when I was playing for the New York Giants. He was a broker and an absolute total sports nutcase. He seemed to be capable of anything, including an instance when we were playing the Pittsburgh Steelers in the Super Bowl. The security was unbelievably tight; no one, and I mean no one, without the purest of credentials, was allowed on the field. I was out before the game doing warmups when I heard, "Hey Fran," and there was Don Engel! I cannot imagine how he got there.

Another time, he came to one of our games in Minnesota, when I was with the Vikings. Nobody was allowed into the Vikings locker room after the game, but sure enough, there he was in the Viking dressing room. I will always remember Don as one of the true legendary characters.

* * *

Marvin Bluestein was the spitting image of Danny DeVito. Marvin was from Brunswick, Georgia. He was a brilliant man, very musically inclined, and was in the shrimp business. He quit his business one day and decided to become an actor. I was able to help him obtain a few auditions. After every audition he had, and there were many, when I asked how it went, he would always tell me the same thing.

"Francis, they loved me," he would say. He never did get an acting gig.

Marvin made everyone around him laugh all the time, and he did it for all the years that I knew him. I miss him. Outside of my family, I don't know that I mourned the loss of anyone more than I did him. He was a true friend and a wonderful person.

And one of my very favorite people is Ruth Brooks. Anyone who doesn't know her is missing out. She may be the best entrepreneur in the world. She runs a little country store up by Lake Burton, Georgia, and I always stop to see her on the way to my lake place.

She works every day and makes dinner for her husband, Bobby Brooks, who is himself a character. You know you must have done something right in your life when the community names a road after you, and Bobby holds that distinction. I think Ruth Brooks owns property everywhere, even though she has only been to Atlanta twice in her life. I always tell her about the places I have recently visited. I might say, "I just got back from Pebble Beach, New York City, or Paris," and she will usually follow with, "I just got back from Wal-Mart, Fran." She never travels but her energy and her intellect are second to none. She is as interesting a person as I know—lively, smart, and always engaged. Ruth Brooks is a real treasure.

> *"When he talks with you, he makes you feel like you are the most important person in the world. I am not the same person when I am not around him."*
>
> —STUART FINESTONE, ATTORNEY AND FRIEND

My family and I travel to St. Barts every year and I can never wait to see a special person. She is the only woman who will ever be in competition with my wife. Her name is Pearl, she is 97 years old, and she loves to swim in the waters there with her daughter, Joan. Both of them are delightful. We also love seeing Barry, a true sun worshiper and one of the most content people on earth.

Back in Atlanta, there's Mr. Ole. That's what everyone calls him, and he is legendary. I met Mr. Ole in the late '70s. He eats out seven days a week; you can always find him somewhere around the Buckhead area of Atlanta.

In the sports arena, I have met some greats like Pete Rozelle, former commissioner of the National Football League from 1960 to

1989. He took the NFL to another level during his time in office. He was an amazing leader and was in many ways responsible for what the game is today.

I have also been fortunate to have met some of the greatest coaches of the past, men like Paul Brown, Vince Lombardi, and Don Shula. Brown may have been the best coach ever. And what Lombardi did in Green Bay likely will never be replicated. I met Shula at the Pro Bowl. The great Johnny Unitas and I were the quarterbacks, and I told Shula, "Don't worry, I'll bail out Johnny for you." I'm glad he knew I was kidding.

Joe Namath may have been my crosstown competition, but he has a good soul and is a nice guy. It is only too bad that the National Football League never saw a healthy Joe Namath. He could throw the football with the best of them.

Few players have ever come along like Paul Hornung. He could run, throw, block, and was even a kicker for the Packers. He won the Heisman Trophy when he was the quarterback at Notre Dame—and the Irish won only two games that year! His talent surfaced among all the losses to still be named the best player in America.

Awe is a powerful word, and one that I don't use lightly, but I am in awe of athletes like Tiger Woods and Michael Jordan. I only met Tiger once, when he was just a child, but I do know Michael Jordan. To watch them both at their game is to be truly awestruck.

More than any athlete, Woods inspires awe in me. He is special. He appeared on *That's Incredible!* at the ripe age of 3. What he has done in the golf world is even more incredible!

There has never been anyone in any sport that handles himself better than he does. And he has dominated a sport in a way that no other person ever has before. He approaches the game with an incredible work ethic. He won the Masters at age 21. No one that young ever wins the Masters because it takes incredible skill and experience to play the course successfully. And not only does Woods win the Masters, but he wins it by *12 strokes!*

Then he comes off the course and that same night tells his golf coach, Butch Harmon, that he wants to change his golf swing. He wins the Masters by a record number of strokes and he wants to change his swing? And he says, I can win golf tournaments, but I want to win *every* golf tournament. This is what drives Tiger Woods, and this is what makes him so special.

Other golfers can't stand up against Woods because he has something inside of him. He is part of the dirt, part of the grass, and part of the club, and part of the ball. It is something that cannot be taught. You cannot teach greatness. You can enable a person to play better, but without greatness you cannot get there. And Tiger is where few will ever be.

Another who is close to Woods' and Jordan's status in my mind is the great Boston Celtic, Bill Russell. He could dominate on the basketball court like few before and after him. Years ago, we did an AT&T commercial together. I'll never forget that I beat him in a foul-shooting contest! Russell has the face of a champion, a big laugh, and a big smile. He could be controversial because he spoke his mind, but it's something I admire in him—in anyone, for that matter.

There are two other tremendous athletes from the NBA from Celtics/Lakers championship runs that I admire, and I also happen to be friends with both of them: John Havlicek and Jerry West. The two of them were extraordinary players and the heroes of my generation. Havlicek molded himself into a great shooter. He was a hard-nosed, determined player. And Jerry West—holy cow! I can think of no better way to describe him than that. I remember watching them when they had West and Elgin Baylor. What a team they were! And then along came Wilt Chamberlain.

I remember once staying at the Jack Tar Hotel when we were playing on the West Coast. Chamberlain happened to be staying there at the same time. We had some free time after Saturday practice and were hanging out in the hotel lobby. A reporter there was on the phone calling up to Wilt Chamberlain's room to confirm a meeting they had scheduled.

If there is one football player that I was truly in awe of, it was Gino Marchetti.

"Wilt, this is Harry here and I have a 2:00 PM appointment with you today. We had agreed to meet in the lobby of the hotel. How will I know you?"

Can you imagine that? Wilt Chamberlain, at least 7"1', clearly the tallest man of his era, and this reporter says, "How will I know you?" Unbelievable! I have never forgotten that.

If there is one football player that I was truly in awe of, it was Gino Marchetti. He stood head and shoulders above the rest. He was the toughest and best defensive end I have ever seen. He had the same drive as Tiger Woods, a motor inside him that never quit.

One of the biggest thrills in my life was to have the opportunity to meet the legendary Bronko Nagurski, thought by some to be the greatest football player who ever lived.

According to an old football legend, former University of Minnesota football coach Clarence Spears was lost and stopped to ask directions to the nearest town, when he discovered Bronko. Nagurski, who had been plowing a field without a horse, lifted his plow and used it to point to the direction of the nearest town. He was signed on the spot to play football for the Gophers.

Bronko played on offense and defense and was an All-American at both positions, fullback and tackle! He played for the Chicago Bears with Red Grange. Once Mick Tingelhoff and I were on a fishing trip with our kids and former Minnesota State Representative

Bob Lessard arranged the meeting. It was unbelievable. *He* was unbelievable! Surprisingly, Bronko was a very soft-spoken guy. When I met him, I asked, "Tell me, how fast was Red Grange?" Bronko looked at me and he quietly said, "I don't know how fast he was, but I do know he was one step slower than me!"

*   *   *

One of the most incredible and amazing people I have met in my lifetime has been Sam Walton. I am a better person for having known him. He has that same drive. He is to me the greatest businessperson who ever lived. Think of what he did! He was a high school graduate from Bentonville, Arkansas, and he had an idea about going out into the world of retail and providing greater value at lower prices. He had to compete with the "big guys" like Sears Roebuck and Montgomery Ward. In fact, he went to Sears Roebuck and Montgomery Ward and told them about his idea—and they threw him out!

So he started Wal-Mart in the 1950s and built it into a gigantic corporation without their help. Now his business employs more people than any company in the world. Mr. Sam died in 1992, but I sure am glad our paths crossed in life. He was special.

As we go through life, everyone has the opportunity to meet interesting people. Some we remember because they had an impact on our lives. Others we remember because of their qualities and perhaps special abilities. I have loved being around people, enjoying them, studying them, learning from them. I take a little part of each of them inside of me wherever I go. These are only a few of the many people who have influenced me.

CHAPTER 12

Every Day
Is Game Day

I wake up every day of my life with the need to validate myself. I am energized and I am driven.

I don't have to go to practice anymore. I don't have to go to evening and weekend meetings to put together a game plan. There are no films to watch and no playbooks to study. Even so, every day for me is still game day. All of the joy and excitement in the game still burns inside of me and motivates me every day.

I love being around people and I am always curious about them, whether I meet them in a business capacity or in my personal life. People fascinate me, and every day they teach me something new.

My companies are built on relationships. Relationships are about trust and trust is about caring. I care about people and my companies do, too.

It's important to me that I surround myself with people I respect and who are respectful. For example, if I am out to dinner with someone who treats the waitstaff or others badly, I don't want to be with them again. Everyone we come into contact with in life deserves a modicum of respect. And I won't accept or tolerate anything less.

"He is a leader in the truest sense of the word. He is always trying to make things in business and in life better for everyone."

—NICK SERBA,
BUSINESS PARTNER AND FRIEND

I am an extremely active and very competitive person. I need to be engaged in something every day. I have built 15 companies in my life and learned a great deal from each of them. And the most important thing I learned is that there is always more to know. And I continue to be that sponge, trying to suck everything out of life that I can absorb.

There was never a time in my high school, collegiate, or professional career when I thought I had all the answers. I learned from the best throughout my whole professional career and even before that. My boyhood heroes like Sammy Baugh and Sid Luckman taught me about greatness and how dreams can become realities. I learned from Bart Starr over in Green Bay and Roger Staubach in Dallas; I asked questions, and I studied what they did. I learned how to be an NFL quarterback from Norm Van Brocklin. I got my information from the masters of their professions, I reached out to them every opportunity that I could. Without that, I'm certain that I would not have been successful.

I often speak about people who have things figured out. People who have it figured out have thought life through. They have looked at the important things in life and understand

> *"Francis had tremendous ability and he constantly worked at it. He knew more about our opponents than anyone I ever knew. He studied the game..."*
>
> —MICK TINGELHOFF

what they are and what they are doing. They are comfortable in their life, in their jobs, with their family, and they have a true balance to their life. Bud Grant had it figured out.

And I'm not sure that you can have life really figured out without animals in your life. I have four dogs and I learn from each one of them every day. They teach me with their instinct, their perception, their loyalty, and their love.

In football, some players just learn by instinct. They figure it out. Maybe there is a player who is not particularly fast, maybe he doesn't have the greatest of skills, but he figures out the game and he makes the plays. And there are all kinds of people and athletes like that.

Consider Roy Winston, our outside linebacker on the Vikings. "Moonie" wasn't the typical pro football prototype linebacker, but he figured out how to play the game. Bobby Bryant, one of our great defensive backs, didn't have all the natural abilities of the others he played with or against, but he played as well as anyone we had. He played for 13 years and made more big plays for the Vikings when I was there than I did as the quarterback. He made more plays than Ahmad Rashad or Alan Page or Jim Marshall. Bryant had the game figured out.

In business, I need to be totally engaged. I know that I am better today at what I do than I was at 18, 28, or 38 years old. And I know that the reason why is because I have never stopped learning.

I got better as a football player because I asked questions. I wanted to know everything about everything. In my early years with the Vikings, I used to go into the administrative offices before practice or on off days to learn about scouting, accounting, ticket sales…absolutely everything. I was interested in every aspect of the operation. I didn't want just to follow the playbook and do what whomever wrote it said to do. I wanted to be involved in the planning, the preparation—everything. Even though I was hurt at the end of my career, I believe that I was still able to play at a high level because I was smarter and better prepared.

And so here in my postfootball life, I have built my businesses from the ground up, from my own ideas, and I bring in the people to assist in the process. I like to hire people and work with them. I still work hard in our businesses every day and I have wonderful people around me. We talk and ask questions and we try to find ways to improve. We never have all the answers, and we never have the best answers because there are always better answers and better questions.

One of the things that I look for in people is a presence and a "face." It's a powerful, meaningful, and important way to evaluate people.

Many years ago, I was sitting in the stands next to Bill Rigney, watching a California Angels workout. Rigney was a scout who had been around Major League Baseball for more than two decades and was a pretty good judge of talent.

He played for the New York Giants baseball franchise from 1946 to 1953, and was an All-Star in 1948. Rigney became the Giants manager from 1956 to 1960, the Los Angeles Angels' first manager in 1961, and also managed the Minnesota Twins from 1970 to 1972. He won American League Manager of the Year honors in 1962 and won the AL West Championship with the Twins in 1970. There is no question that he knew something about ballplayers.

There is something about a person's face that can give a good indication of their character. Jim Marshall. Bud Grant. They have a face and a presence.

We were sitting in the stands watching the players on the field, and I noticed one player in particular and asked, "Tell me about this guy." And he turned to me and said, "I wish he had a better face." I had no idea what he meant. He continued, "Well, you know, he throws good, he fields good, he runs good, he hits good, but he just doesn't have that *face*. He doesn't have the extra drive, that extra connection to make him a great player. He doesn't have that special look about him."

Over the years as I have looked back on the conversation with Bill Rigney and the player's accomplishments over what ended up being a fairly significant career in Major League Baseball, and he was right. He was a good player with exceptional skills, but never a great player. Some people say that people like that don't have the X-factor. It starts with the heart and it goes from there, and the face is a part of it.

Sometimes I sit in hotel lobbies with my daughter, watching people and reading faces. And my daughter has become a face reader. There is something about a person's face that can give a good indication of their character. Jim Marshall. Bud Grant. They have a face and a presence.

*   *   *

My life is about relationships. My friend and lawyer, Stuart Finestone, who has an office across the hall from mine in Atlanta, is as great a friend as I have. We eat lunch together almost every day. We talk about everything and I learn a lot from him. I would do anything for him and he would do anything for me.

I am a serial entrepreneur and I always have been. I am constantly into something. I have worked all of my life. Someone said to me one day, "Fran, why do you do this? Why do you drive yourself every day? You have a great family, a great home,

> *"He has a magnetic, infectious personality that attracts people to him. And the attraction is not from his celebrity status...but rather to him as a person.... He has a fascinating zeal for everything he is involved in."*
>
> —Dr. Dan Barrow,
> Chairman, Deptartment of
> Neurosurgery, Emory University

solid businesses, financial security, and yet you work so hard every day. Why do you do this?" My response was, "*What would I do?*"

There is a part in the movie *Frost/Nixon* in which Richard Nixon talks about retired people being miserable, bored, and purposeless. At that very moment I watched it, it hit me. It was as if I had an epiphany. It was so clear: my life is not about that. I could never do that. I can't just stop working and find a way to get through the day.

I wake up every day of my life with the need to validate myself. I am energized and I am driven. I give a lot of credit to my brother Dallas. When we were growing up, it was always a challenge for me to keep up with him. He was bigger, stronger, faster, and our age difference meant that I would have to work harder to compete with him. It taught me about proving myself and meeting any of the challenges put in front of me.

Every day is game day for me. And the fire in my belly is the same as it was in the back alleys of Washington, D.C., or on the field at Met Stadium. And the relationship part is the critical element present that makes it all worthwhile. My life has been about those relationships, in my football life, in my business life, and in my personal life. I could not have accomplished what I have in my life without great teammates, great partners, great associates, and a great family.

"Fran thrives on using his knowledge to assist others."

—Scott Miller,
business associate and friend

I have worked my entire life and I value that greatly. When I was only five years old, I had a little red wagon and I would go into the grocery store and offer to take the little old ladies' groceries from the store to their homes. That was in 1945, and I would earn a nickel or a dime for it. It was my very first job.

At seven, I had a paper route. I delivered newspapers every afternoon during the week and at 6:00 AM on Saturdays and Sundays.

I used to think in my younger life that the CEOs, the guys who ran the big companies, were the best, the ones to emulate. But now I know that the "best" are the ones who build their own companies. People like Bill Gates, the college dropout, or Michael Dell from Dell Business Systems, who has just one-quarter of college under his belt.

When I left football, I didn't want to go back. I took all I learned from football and applied it to my business world. None of the companies I built were easy. I built them all from the ground up. But I brought the planning, the preparing, the studying, and mostly the passion. I have as much passion for my business life as I ever had for football.

Other byproducts from football, fundamentals and discipline, have been crucial in my business life. You have to have the fundamentals down and you have to be to be disciplined in your business life just as much, maybe more, than in football. I have known plenty of entrepreneurs who are not disciplined. They are the ones falling for each next get-rich-quick scheme. I believe to be successful in football or in business you must have sound fundamentals, and you have to be disciplined.

Sam Walton built his business on a solid foundation: value. I learned so much from him. He created value for a customer. He did not do it with smoke and mirrors; he did it by caring about the customer. If there is one thing that I've learned about business, it is that if you are going to be successful, you have to make sure your products or services are of value to the consumer. You also have to be sure that the people you are working with are ethical and that they also care about the customer.

When I played football, I looked forward to every game just like I now look forward to coming to work every day. But coming to work or playing a football game is much more than simply arriving to play the game. It takes passion and it takes preparation. I understand both and I have both.

I am often asked what it was like to play at the old Metropolitan Stadium in the cold of winter. Bud Grant never let us have heaters on the sideline or wear gloves. How did we survive? Preparation.

It was easy to get ready for a game within Bud's framework. I loved playing under those conditions. We had an advantage over other teams when the conditions were brutal because we prepared better.

I thought about what I was going to wear. I experimented to figure out what would work for me. I didn't want to be so bundled up that I couldn't move, so I would cut the sleeves off of my thermal gear. I wanted the warmth around my body but I wanted my arms and legs free to move. I cut the thermal pants so they didn't go all the way down so I could run freely. I always made sure that I was warm enough, but still maintained the proper flexibility.

I was never cold in the games and never cold on the sideline. I was prepared. It was easy. It merely took adjusting to the conditions. From there, it became a mindset, a discipline. You don't let the cold bother you. You don't let the wind, the rain, or the snow bother you. You have confidence in your ability to prepare and to succeed.

*   *   *

I have met a couple entrepreneurs who have come to me and told me about their projects. They have been developing them for two or three years, and they both have come to me separately, saying, "It's taken a lot longer and has taken a lot more money than I thought it would. I thought by now we would have executed our exit strategy." I said, "What are you talking about, *exit strategy?*"

They both said, "Well, you know, we were going to raise money and build these products and then as soon as we had that done, we were going to sell it for millions of dollars."

Businessmen like that make me angry. They don't care about the company; they're just interested in making a quick buck. That's pretty foolhardy, quite frankly, and those two found out that it is not that easy to find somebody to put millions of dollars into your deal, do a few gimmicky things, and expect someone to come along and buy it for hundreds of millions of dollars. That was the Internet bubble, and we saw what happened. That was a dream world! And it won't happen again.

Real entrepreneurs find products or services that make sense, put a plan together, and perform the adjustments to make it work. At least that's what I do and I have been very successful at it.

When you try to bring new ideas and innovations, or new products and new ways to bring growth to your business, you often encounter people who will try to find every reason why it won't work. We run across stumbling blocks in business and in life. But persistence and discipline are what create success.

I am 69 years old. I have created my own wealth and I don't have to do this every day. But the fact is, for me, I do have to do this because it is the right thing to do. No one will make things happen for you.

In football, we often were underdogs. We went into games when no one believed we had a chance to win. In 1961 against the Chicago Bears, they said we had no chance. In the Giants' opening game in 1969 against the Vikings, they said we had no chance! I don't believe in the "no chance" concept.

There may be roadblocks and hurdles in front of you, but you have to persevere. You have to push forward. And if you do that, you will break through. You will have a chance. And you will get to where you want to get if you go after it and make your own success.

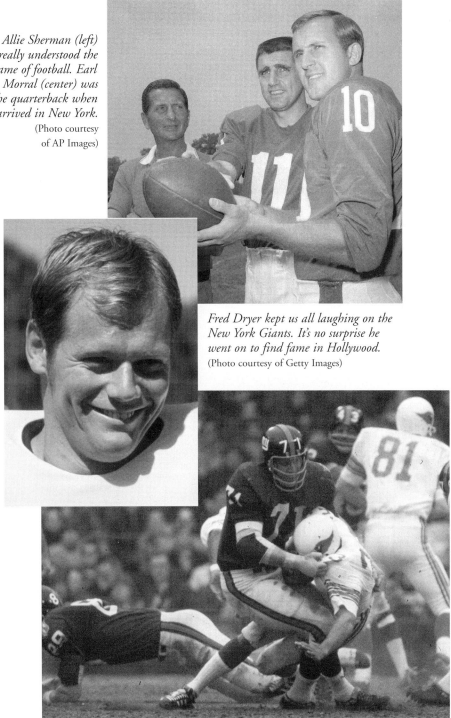

Allie Sherman (left) really understood the game of football. Earl Morral (center) was the quarterback when I arrived in New York. (Photo courtesy of AP Images)

Fred Dryer kept us all laughing on the New York Giants. It's no surprise he went on to find fame in Hollywood. (Photo courtesy of Getty Images)

I first met "Benchwarmer" Bob Lurtsema while playing for the New York Giants. I would later reunite with him back on the Minnesota Vikings. (Photo courtesy of Getty Images)

I never intended to be a scrambling quarterback in the professional ranks, but that's just what happened. I never lacked the resolve to put forth anything less than an all-out effort to win, whatever it took. (Photo courtesy of the Minnesota Vikings)

Jerry Burns is the funniest man I have ever known and a brilliant, exceptional football coach, and offensive coordinator.
(Photo courtesy of the Minnesota Vikings)

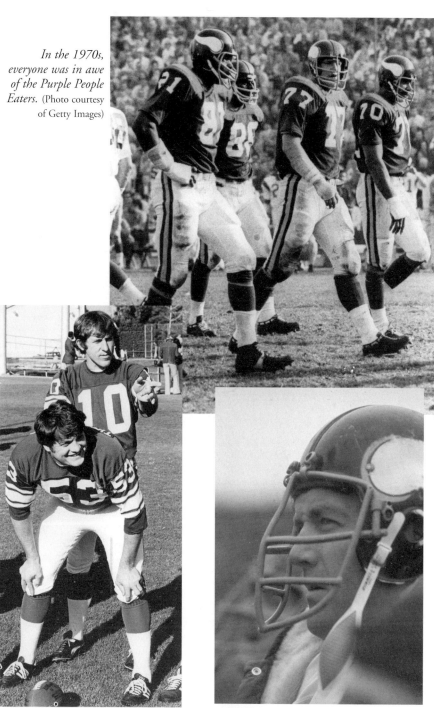

In the 1970s, everyone was in awe of the Purple People Eaters. (Photo courtesy of Getty Images)

Mick Tingelhoff is one of the greatest players I have had the privilege to play alongside. (Photo courtesy of the Minnesota Vikings)

One of my best friends from my playing days is Grady Alderman. He played in the trenches for the Minnesota Vikings for 14 years, and is as solid a football player as they come. (Photo courtesy of Getty Images)

*Once Chuck Foreman
arrived, our offense was
firing on all cylinders.*
(Photo courtesy of the
Minnesota Vikings)

*I was born with an
incredible desire and
competitive spirit to
win, no matter what.*
(Photo courtesy of the
Minnesota Vikings)

Bud Grant is probably the single-most influential person I have met. I learned so much from him. (Photo courtesy of the Tarkenton family)

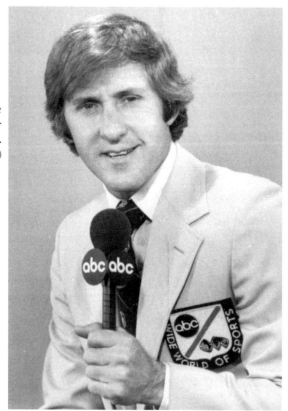

After leaving football, I did a tour of duty as a commentator for Monday Night Football. (Photo courtesy of AP Images)

And another as a co-host on That's Incredible! *(pictured here with John Davidson and Cathy Lee Crosby).* (Photo courtesy of the Tarkenton family)

One of my greatest thrills in life was when my son Matthew and I met the legendary Bronko Nagurski, thought by some to be the greatest football player that ever lived. (Photo courtesy of the Tarkenton family)

Being inducted into the Pro Football Hall of Fame remains an indescribable honor. (Photo courtesy of the Minnesota Vikings)

The Brothers Tarkenton (left to right): me, Dallas, and Wendell. (Photo courtesy of the Tarkenton family)

My family is, and always was, the most important thing in my life. (Photo courtesy of the Tarkenton family)

CHAPTER 13

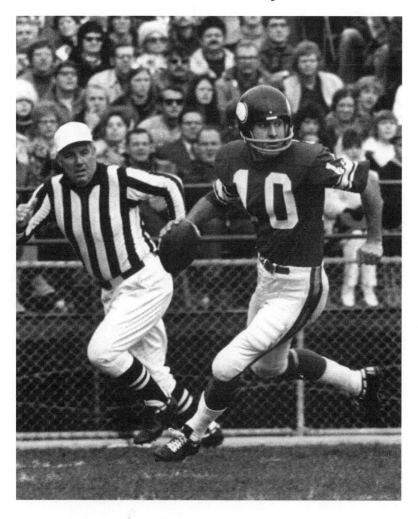

The Big Picture

When you can put faces, signs, reality, trust, caring, and relationships into the foundation of what you build your life on, you have a good chance to succeed.

Remember Bud Grant and the players at training camp in Mankato, walking across the freshly seeded grass? Remember how some of them who walked across the grass didn't see the "signs"?

Remember the ballplayer who was a good player but didn't have the "face" to be a great player?

The "face" and the "signs" are significant ingredients for success in sports, business, and in life.

Signs are everywhere. I went to a business meeting a while back with the idea that one of my companies might do business with another company. After the meeting, there was no question in my mind or those of my staff that we would not do business with them. Why? The signs were everywhere. We didn't like their approach. We didn't like the people. They were arrogant. They were self-absorbed. Most importantly, they did not represent what was important to us. Reading the signs made our decision easy.

Signs provide guidance and direction for us. I am constantly on the lookout for signs. I always want to keep myself in a position to assume nothing and question everything. I often think about the banking industry. How could those companies have gotten themselves into the mess they are in? People believe in banks. They are supposed to be stable and dependable. How did it happen? The answer is simple. They didn't see the signs when they were right in front of them.

You have to be out in front of things at all times, looking for signs. It is extremely important to look carefully into every situation or circumstance and see the reality of what is before you. Parents who have children who are veering off course often get caught up in day-to-day activities and miss the signs. They may miss the cues that their child is using drugs, hanging with the wrong crowd of friends, or missing school. The signs are always there but parents too often miss them.

Some years ago, I had a friend talk to me about his son. He told me that he was suspicious that his son was in some kind of trouble. But he told me that he had a long conversation with his son and was positively convinced that everything was fine. But he asked me to talk to him, too.

There was trouble, no question about it, and I told my friend so. There were signs everywhere; he just missed them. It was because my friend was too close to the problem and didn't look hard enough.

There are so many people who think they have all the answers. No one does, but some they think they do. And when people think they have all the answers, they lose their edge. They start making errors of assumption. They don't bother to look for the signs or question what they see in front of them. They don't search for the correct answers.

This entire country has been hurt by a loss of vision by not looking for signs. Corporate greed has corroded people's trust in business, and now even our most sacred institutions are failing.

Bud Grant taught me by example. He is always looking for the signs. It is looking at reality. It is not what you want it to be. It is about what it *is*!

And when you can put faces, signs, reality, trust, caring, and relationships into the foundation of what you build your life on, you have a good chance to succeed.

Brad Carr and his story changed my life. It came to me, I don't know why. But I was lucky enough to have it in front of me, and the wherewithal to do something about it. It was a powerful experience. Had I not acted on it, I would not have had the pleasure of that act. It helped me to realize how good I could feel about something, how interested I could become about something, and the effect I could have by solving a problem for someone else.

If you look for the signs, they will tell you where to go and where not to go. Signs are a part of reality. And realities in life may include failures. It does not bother me to look at the reality of my failures; we can always learn from them.

I look at my failure to go along with Jerry Burns on the crucial third-down play in the 1975 Dallas game. If we had made the first down, we win the game. There would not have been a Hail Mary pass. There would not have been a season-ending play. We would have kept the ball and won the game; there is no doubt in my mind. We would probably go on that year and win the Super Bowl; it was our best Viking team. And we would have won the Super Bowls that followed. And history in the NFL is changed forever. All because of that one little play.

But because I can look at the reality of my failures I can accept that it didn't happen that way. Does that make sense? It should because there is a difference here. You can be devastated by a choice in your life and wish that you had made a different decision, but you should also be able to accept your failures. And I have been able to do that. Looking at evaluating your failures is simply another opportunity of looking at the signs and learning from the experience.

*   *   *

The most important skill we can learn in our lifetime is how to solve problems. We face them every day. They are always in front of us. And a problem cannot be solved unless it is identified first.

As we look at the big picture for our future and that of our economy, we too often do not want to look at reality. We don't want to see how things really are. If we look at the financial meltdown that happened, there is plenty to learn from. The more information that we get, the more it becomes clear that it did not just happen overnight. It has been coming for years and years and years. Our financial minds on Wall Street, on Main Street, or in Congress, financial experts in America and in Europe—they had to have seen this coming. But they didn't.

People spent money like crazy because financial geniuses around the globe saw the signs but ignored them. The politicians saw the signs but ignored them. And consumers, though without the same scope of understanding, saw the signs and ignored them. It's another lesson for us. Bad news doesn't get better with age. In all of our lives, in everything we do, we have to look at the reality of what is going on around us and not discount it.

If our kids are using drugs, we cannot ignore it; we have to deal with it. We have to look at the reality of whatever our situation is because that is the only way we can make a difference. If we are spending more money than we have and our budget is out of balance, we have to deal with it.

Whether it is a problem affecting us all or one that is pertinent to an individual, large or small, the signs identify it, define the magnitude of it, and help us to solve the problem.

Because of this, I have had success in business. I manage every single detail. I have my fingers in everything. I know what's going on. I look for signs. I don't leave things to chance. I have a burning desire in my heart and soul to makes things better today than they were yesterday. I have this same desire today in everything I do.

*   *   *

I would have to think that most people are interested in peak performance, whether it be individually, as a team, or as a business. How do we, in the most stressful situations, perform at the highest level? I think this is one of the great challenges that we face in life.

There is no question that the model for us to look at is in sports. We have watched Tiger Woods over the years and marveled at how he can make putts of any length when the pressure is on.

We watched Michael Phelps win more gold medals than any other athlete in the history of the Olympics. He was able to swim against the greatest swimmers in the world under tremendous pressure.

We have doubt within all of us, and doubt can erode positive energies. When we have doubt, we question ourselves. When we question ourselves, we are not able to perform because those energies, rather than being positive energies, can turn negative. We start making excuses.

Jerry Jones, owner of the Dallas Cowboys, once told a story about making a big commitment to a quarterback who had been challenged with drugs, and all kinds of off-the-field problems, who was never really able to perform to the level of his ability. One day he invited the great heavyweight boxing champion, George Foreman, to practice.

> *We have doubt within all of us, and doubt can erode positive energies.*

Jones asked George if he thought his quarterback was going to make it. George said simply, "Nope." Jerry asked him why. And George said, "He spits the bit when he gets on the big stage. He finds excuses. And when you start looking for excuses and you spit the bit, you don't perform."

George then told Jerry about his first heavyweight boxing championship. He was in the ring before the match, when the boxers get nose-to-nose, glove-to-glove, and eyeball-to-eyeball, trying to intimidate each other, and he looked into the eyes of his opponent. He could tell that his competition had already spit the bit. When he looked into his eyes, he knew it was already over.

And the difference here is not always in the ability of people. It is our ability to control our emotions and our energies. Doubt lingers in all of us, but we can actually will the doubt out.

No matter what your stage is, it's your big stage right? Whether it is in business, in life, or sports. When you get on the stage that you are playing on, that is the biggest stage in the world. You cannot let doubt overcome you. You must take that doubt and make it positive energy. Because that is what the great ones do.

*   *   *

Over the years, there have been a lot of NFL quarterbacks. However, few play for that many seasons. It seems as though every year there is significant conversation surrounding the league's quarterbacks. It seems that there are just never enough quarterbacks of quality that teams can depend on. It was the same way in my day.

I was listening to a quarterback on ESPN recently. He had been a No. 1 draft pick and he bombed out. He played for a few years, was picked up as a free agent with one team, and then ended up with still another. He said on ESPN that he was 29 years old and "If only they had taught me better…" He said they never taught him how to play quarterback!

I believe the coaches and the scouts in pro football do not understand the quarterback position, nor have they ever understood the quarterback position. Bill Walsh was a brilliant quarterback coach, a great offensive coach, and he made average quarterbacks become outstanding. He coached Steve DeBerg into becoming a really great quarterback. He took Joe Montana, a third-round draft choice from Notre Dame (and remember, when you are taken in the third round of the NFL Draft, they don't think you can play) and Bill made him immortal.

When Steve Young came out of Utah, and he was a runner not a quarterback, people didn't think he could play. Yet Walsh made him into a great quarterback. But there are not many coaches, not many systems that can do these two things: evaluate the quarterback and coach the quarterback. And this has been true forever.

So how *do* you evaluate a quarterback in the National Football League? It's not easy.

Alex Smith, just a few years ago, was the first pick of the draft. In his third year as quarterback, he was injured and lost his starting job. Joey Harrington was the third overall pick in the draft and has not lived up to expectations. Ryan Leaf was the second pick in the draft, and was out of football in a handful of years. Everyone thought that there was extraordinary talent and they were proved wrong.

Johnny Unitas wasn't even drafted. He was a free agent and was cut by two NFL teams before ending up in Baltimore. Bart Starr was a 17th-round draft choice. Brett Favre, drafted and traded; no one saw his potential. Tom Brady of the New England Patriots, maybe today's best quarterback, was a sixth-round draft choice from Michigan. Somebody thought he wasn't strong enough, fast enough, or a good enough passer. And to think, if Drew Bledsoe hadn't been injured, Tom Brady might have never played.

So the bottom line here is this: the people who evaluate quarterbacks, in my estimation, don't understand the position. They don't see the signs.

On the other hand, I don't think you can make a quarterback great. That comes from within. Peyton Manning is phenomenal because Peyton Manning wants to be the best, and he works at it. He has the work ethic. He has trained for the position and he has studied it. He has a feel for the position, and it is a part of him.

And I think to be successful at the quarterback position in the National Football League, you must have skills and something present on the inside. It is something that others don't have, that separates the great from those who can't make it.

You must have the fundamentals, you must have a strong system, and you have to have an offensive coach who understands the passing game—and not very many really do. But in the end, the great ones become themselves. And all of the great ones are different.

With 32 professional football teams, I think there are only two great quarterbacks playing the game today: Peyton Manning and Tom Brady. They stand head and shoulders above the rest. But their approach is different and they are fundamentally different. And isn't is also amazing that after all these years and all the sophistication that has gone into scouting and evaluating players, the quarterback position is basically light years away from being understood?

Football today, as you look at the big picture, doesn't *get it* in many respects. The wrong approach is taken to the game. The same films are looked at, the same plays are looked at, and the positive attack of the opponent is balanced with the negative side like, *how are we going to prevent turnovers?*, instead of, *how are we going to make first downs? How do we get mismatches on the defenses? How do we outflank them? How do we get my best receiver over here to be with their weakest defender? How do you get Alan Page over there against their weakest lineman?* It doesn't happen like it should.

I played a few years so I think I know something about being a quarterback, throwing the football, and running an offense. I have been a high school quarterback, a college quarterback, and a pro quarterback. That's a lot of years taking the snap from center. And enough people thought I played the position and the game well enough to elect me into the College Football Hall of Fame and the Pro Football Hall of Fame.

I have been retired from football for more than 30 years and not one single coach, player, scout, or anyone connected with the game at the grade school, high school, college, or professional level has ever asked me a single question about playing quarterback, passing the football, running an offense, or anything connected to the game. I find this so odd. I built my career as a sponge; how could this be?

Back in the days when Dallas was having success, I would call my friend Don Meredith, the Cowboys quarterback. I would ask him, "What are you guys doing? Tell me what you are doing." When Bart Starr was beating everyone over in Green Bay, I would do the same. I spent hours on the phone with the old quarterbacks learning whatever I could from them. I would absolutely exhaust Sid Luckman when he would come to see me before the games in Chicago. Why wouldn't I? I wanted to know what he thought about everything!

I would have an idea about something and I would ask the old greats of the game, "Tell me what is stupid about my idea. Tell me why this won't work." I wanted to know! I would challenge them. I wanted them to give me their knowledge, their opinions, and their expertise.

I have built my business knowledge the same way. Ask questions. Solve problems! Business is no different than sports.

> "*Fran has tremendous enthusiasm for everything he does...He continues to be a student every single day. He always wants to learn more about everything he does.*"
> —RICH GAROFALO,
> FRIEND AND BUSINESS PARTNER

You have to figure it out and you never get it totally figured out. You have to learn today and be better than yesterday.

Coaches today in many respects have stopped learning. The best coaches may be the high school coaches because many of them likely acknowledge that they haven't figured it all out.

I don't have all the answers but I am willing to find them. Someone has them or parts of them. And you have to go looking for solutions. And that's what makes life so interesting.

I never wanted to own a team or be a general manager. They have too many headaches. I have much more fun doing what I am doing. I like being in control and influencing the outcome of things. That's impossible as a general manager and coach, when all you can do is watch what is happening on the field.

My friend and former NFL quarterback great Joe Theismann was once asked what kind of coach I would have been, to which he responded, "Well, Fran wouldn't have been able to coach one of the teams because he would have had to coach *all* of the teams."

Some think at 50 or 60 years of age we should retire—play golf, walk the beach, take a lot of naps. That simply won't work for me. No offense meant to those who enjoy this, but I don't understand it. I feel the most fulfilled when I am working and solving problems.

I go after problems in life. In football, I went after Mike Lynn when he wanted to release Ahmad Rashad from our roster. I stepped up to the plate and said my piece. I know who I am and what I have to do. I love to work with people and love trying to help people. I have a big heart. I know inside who I am and what is important to me. I know how I feel about things. I am comfortable in my own skin.

I believe it is going to be the Boone Pickens of the world, the people who are not afraid to speak their mind and buck convention—people like you and me who fully understand the power of the people—who are going to bring about the changes, and the politicians will follow.

We cannot keep drinking the Kool-Aid of the politicians; they have proven that they don't have the answers.

We have to be responsible in what we do and ride out these bad cycles because in a free market economy we will continue to have highs and lows, and we need to understand that and stay the course. This is true in sports, it is true in business, and it is true in life. Recognizing and understanding this is the start, and adjusting and solving the problems that develop along the way is the solution. But we must have the spirit and the will to want to do that, and then do it.

"His generosity is more than anyone could possibly believe. I cannot imagine working for anyone else."

—JILL BLITCH, EXECUTIVE ASSISTANT

We each have our own issues to work with and live with every day. My advice is to look for the signs, develop the relationships, solve the problems, look for the solutions, ask the questions, absorb the answers, and have fun in the process. Life is too short to have it any other way.

CHAPTER 14

An Entrepreneur

Business is about people, and that is what rewards me every day. I hire my staff because they are good people. I want to be around those who have good hearts and good souls.

*I*f *football taught me anything about business, it is that you win the game one play at a time.*

People don't change their behavior unless it makes a difference for them to do so.

None of us really pushes hard enough.

Success is the willingness to strive for something you really want. The person who is not reaching the top is no less a success than the one who achieves it, if they both lost blood, sweat, and tears to overcome their obstacles and fears. The failure to be perfect does not make someone any less of a success.

These statements comprise a major part of my belief system.

I didn't come from a wealthy family. I had to work for everything I have. And I have worked my whole life. My dad worked hard, my mother worked hard, my siblings worked hard, too. My parents taught me as much about hard work as anyone.

Even though I'm no longer playing professional football, work still keeps my energy level at a peak. I don't need crowd noise or applause any longer. The business world is my arena now, and I love every minute of it.

There may not be the same instant gratification in business that often happens in professional football, but there is problem solving every single day. It's shoveling and shoveling and working hard, and finally being able to say, "Wow! We did something really special here." I get a kick out of being able to say that.

I don't think I'll ever be too old for the entrepreneur lifestyle. I love it! Look at the great businessmen of today. Many are over 80 years old and still going. Warren Buffett may be the greatest, smartest investor in the last 30 years. Rupert Murdoch is nealy 80 years old. He built a network, Fox News, from nothing. He knew what he was doing and he went right by CBS, NBC, ABC, and CNN. He obtained the rights to NFL Football and the ratings speak for themselves. He also went out and got *American Idol* when others passed on it, and then afterward people wanted him to get rid of Simon Cowell, but he made the decision to keep him. A good decision, I think. A good businessman follows his instincts.

> *"Fran is still playing the game every day...He is passionate about everything and loves politics, sports, his family, friends, and his business associates."*
>
> —MARK BROWN,
> BUSINESS PARTNER AND FRIEND

If you have fire in your belly, age only stokes it. You become older and wiser! You know more! You combine the fire with age, and it makes for a wonderful ride.

I always ask myself how I can gain advantage over my competition. I don't want a fair advantage. I want an *unfair* one. When we played the Green Bay Packers I wanted to beat them because we prepared better, we worked harder, and we studied harder so that we knew them better than they knew us.

The first time we beat the Packers, they were much better than we were, no question about it. They were the Packers of the '60s: Lombardi, Starr, Hornung, Taylor. We had no chance to win, but we did. Van Brocklin put a game plan together that was just brilliant. And I took that plan of Van Brocklin's and had good success with it against the Packers even after Van Brocklin and I had parted ways. Did we always beat them? No, but we had the elements in place to do it. I learned from Van Brocklin that I always want to have that type of preparation now in the business world.

I am a multitasker. I can't stand being idle or passive, which is why I was unhappy on television. I am not satisfied with limitations. Reading a script or describing what I am seeing is full of limitations. There was no challenge to it.

We are now running two businesses out of my Atlanta offices, two companies that I built from the ground up. We have another we started that is going well also. And I'd take on a dozen more! I am having a great time doing it because it is all about relationships. Business is about people, and that is what rewards me every day. I hire my staff because they are good people. I want to be around those who have good hearts and good souls.

Not just people who do the job, but those who are excited about what they do and want to get better every day.

I want to be around business people who look at reality, those who look at the facts and the data. In many cases, people are not willing to look at the realities. They want to get up every morning and see that the sky is

"Fran Tarkenton is a spectacular businessman who is a student of business, finance, and marketing...He is passionate, has strong opinions, is very humorous, and a wonderful storyteller."

—GARY NORDHEIMER,
BUSINESS PARTNER AND FRIEND

blue, even when it isn't. And if you don't look at realities, the bad numbers, or whatever it is that's present, there is going to be trouble ahead. Some actually think maybe if they just ignore this problem, it will disappear.

Bad news most certainly does not get better with age. Businesspeople who are going to be successful must look at the details of every aspect of what they are doing, and not through rose-colored glasses.

I believe entrepreneurs are the best businesspeople in the world—there is no doubt in my mind—because they are the ones who are doing the work. They have their hands all over their business. They have good hearts and they work hard at what they do.

One of the greatest entrepreneurs and human beings I have ever known is Buddy Koffman. Sometimes we are fortunate in our lives to meet people at the right time who have a profound impact on us. Koffman was special. He and his wife, Ruthanne, have been in my life since I was 27 years old. Over the years, he has bought more than 50 businesses. He was in on the early development of Las Vegas, the El Conquistador Hotel in San Juan, and was one of the first to bring the Subaru to America. He has business ventures across the country in industries from amusement parks to liquor distribution.

Buddy is in his office at 7:30 AM every day, enthusiastic and vibrant. He has that fire in his belly. He has taught me a lot about the kind of businessman I want to be.

Twenty years ago, we didn't have a lot of people doing business into their eighties. Now football coaches like Joe Paterno, Bobby Bowden, and John Gagliardi are still at it! John McCain ran for the presidency in his seventies. I surely won't be the one to tell any of them that they are too old to be doing what they are doing. I won't tell Koffman that, either, because at 83 he is better today at what he does than he was when he was 53, 43, or 33 because he has been engaged—and he has learned every step of the way.

*   *   *

Fear is a good thing. When I played high school and college sports and throughout my 18 years in the National Football League, I had those "butterflies in my stomach" that are so often talked about. That fear can come from not knowing what exactly to expect, and it awakens our senses. Having butterflies put me in the right zone. I was ready to get out there and play because my senses were heightened. Fear energizes the senses and brings about confidence.

In today's world, people are fearful of what lies ahead. We are scared of the unknown. Is another shoe in the economy going to drop? Is there more bad news coming? What has happened is that we have all gotten back to our senses. When gas prices got too high, we drove less. We eat out less, we watch our spending. We look at our budgets and say that we cannot spend more than what we have.

In the society that we live in today with constant changes facing us, being able to adapt to the circumstances will get us on the right track. When it was cold

> *"When he dropped back to pass, left the pocket, and started to run, it wasn't the same as when other quarterbacks did it. With Tarkenton, there never seemed to be a worry."*
>
> —MARK THIELEN, LONGTIME FAN

at the old Metropolitan Stadium in Minnesota, I adapted the clothing that I wore. When we were facing a team that was good against the run, we threw short passes at them. When Bud Grant knew we could win the game with our defense, we played a more conservative offensive game.

Once when I was with the New York Giants, we were playing a game at Harvard against the Boston Patriots. It was a cold and miserable day. The conditions were absolutely brutal! The wind was blowing at 30 to 40 miles per hour, and it was almost impossible to throw a pass of longer than 10 yards with any accuracy. So what did we do?

I knew *exactly* what we were going to do. I was not going to throw a pass in that game longer than 10 yards, and I didn't. I threw screen passes, I dumped the ball off to our tight ends, I threw little short passes out in the flat—nothing in the game longer than 10 yards. And we won the game by, I think, three touchdowns.

I've always felt that when the conditions are bad, I can adapt. I did it against the Patriots and I do it in business. Adapting is how I function.

*   *   *

Business principles are pretty basic but so very important. Believe in your products and your services. It is the only way you can have enthusiasm and passion about them. The whole notion of business is the same as life.

Care about the people you are working with and the customers you have acquired. And you must want to make sure that you are doing the right thing by them.

There are no silver bullets. There is no such thing as a get-rich-quick opportunity—unless you're talking about the lottery, and everyone knows those odds. Be wary of anyone who tells you otherwise. This concept is what hinders the entrepreneur on a daily basis. Some have no resistance to it and fall into the trap. Usually these schemes are frauds because they can't deliver what they say they are going to do. But they look good on the surface and yet they have no substance to them.

So how do you overcome these kinds of fantasies? You do it by focusing on relationships and reality. What are the concepts and beliefs? It's about relationships, reality, trust, caring, the signs, and an almost insatiable desire to question and learn.

I am always looking for good ideas. Years ago, in the age of paper ticketing, I came up with the idea to sell advertising space on the jackets of airline tickets. I went to Delta Airlines and told them I would print the ticket jackets for them at no cost. Other airlines were interested, too. I then gave a printer in Chicago half the business to print the jackets. Now all I had to do was get the advertising. I worked hard at it and managed to sell all the ads...except for one blip. Nothing comes easy.

Exxon Corporation had committed to a certain number of ads. The competition for the space was dropped and then they backed out of the deal. I went to New York to pay them a visit. I'm a fighter and a tough guy when I have to be. I don't like people who take advantage of me—especially after making a commitment. When I walked into the board room they had their 20 lawyers waiting for me, sitting around this big conference table. They were ready for me. And I came alone.

I had a little tobacco in my mouth, and I spit a little, made it look like I wasn't too excited but was confident and sure of what I was doing, and said to them, "If you aren't going to live up to your deal, I am going to hold a press conference in Los Angeles and I am going to tell everyone…" And with that, we closed the deal. Sometimes just a little fight is all you need.

I recall a game against the Detroit Lions during my last season. We needed to beat them to win the division championship. In the first half, we were running a split-T formation option play. (I don't know why Jerry Burns put the play in when I was 38 years old, but he did.) Detroit had a good defensive player named Dave Pureifory. I came down the line of scrimmage and pitched the ball to Chuck Foreman and Pureifory never hesitated, he slammed straight into me and crushed me. There was blood all over the place. I needed stitches and my face was a mess.

When I came back to the line of scrimmage, I was absolutely crazed. I went after him and the Lions players yelling and screaming. I raved, "We are going to snap the ball on two, and I am going to drop back seven yards, and I will be right there for you. You think you are so tough, well come and get me!"

I got back to the huddle and Mick Tingelhoff asked me what I'd said. I told him that I'd given the Lions our snap count. "You told them the snap count!?" "Yes," I said, "and this is what we are going to run and you guys are going to protect me."

And we snapped the ball on two, I dropped back the seven yards and stood just where I said I was going to be. I hit Bob Tucker over the middle with a pass before they got to me, and the game was over. After that, they never showed up. I did exactly what I told them I was going to do.

As I said, I am a fighter and I don't back down, but even with the heat of all that was going on in those games and moments, it was always fun for me.

"He always wanted to make something special happen [on the field], and he is the same in business today."

—GRADY ALDERMAN

Another time, we were playing the Rams and they had the great defensive end Jack Youngblood. It was one of the championship games and the field was absolutely frozen.

I threw an interception, and afterward Youngblood came over to me and said, "Hey, way to go, Frannie Boy, way to go! Thanks for the interception!" I have a hard time forgetting things like that. I didn't like his remarks, and I was bound and determined to make him pay for them.

We were ahead late in the game. I converted a pass to one of our running backs on a huge third-down play. On the next play, I knelt down to let the clock run out. I look up and Youngblood is coming across the line, trying to get at me. He runs into Mick and Ed White, our great offensive guard, and they stop him. Youngblood is yelling and screaming and hollering—he is very upset.

We have to run one more play for the game to end. After the snap, I'm able to stay out of his way, and time runs out.

In those days, we never socialized with the other team after the game—*never!* We didn't even shake hands. So as the team is running off the field, I see Jack about 10 yards away. I position myself so I am directly in his line of vision and holler to him, "Hey Jack, Merry Christmas!" and at the same time give him a very unkind gesture with my middle finger as I ran to the locker room. It probably wasn't the Christmas present he was looking for but I certainly loved it!

Competition defines me. I put everything I had into every game (and I do it now, running my businesses). I loved the victories and I suffered with the losses. Losses were very hard on me. I didn't want to go out for dinner, didn't want to be around anyone, and I went into a shell. On Mondays, I started the healing process and got ready for the next game. It was much more than just a job for me. I truly lived it.

The Super Bowl losses were devastating to me; I really suffered with each of them. But to this day, I would have to say the 1975 playoff loss to the Dallas Cowboys was the worst of them all. And you know, by now, all of the reasons.

We are facing tough times today in the business world and in our personal lives. Reading the newspapers, watching the television networks, it seems like no news is good news. It is easy to get discouraged. But I say this is a time for the tough-minded. We cannot give in to the conditions of today.

In the business world, we need to redouble our efforts. We should work harder than ever. It may be a time for you to strive while others are down, but the results may get others back up. These are challenging times and the future is in front of us, and we have to decide how we are going to handle it. We need to examine our personal and professional lives and see if there is a way to do things differently.

I love the people that I am around, love the challenges and the problems of today and tomorrow, and when the day is over, I know I am better, smarter, wiser, and happier than the day before.

CHAPTER 15

Loves and Passions

I really love life. I live it fully and I do it unabashedly. I love my family, my wife, my children, my grandchildren, my friends, and my dogs.

I have passion for most things I do and a great love for people. My family, my friends, and my business associates are more important to me than anything. In addition to that, in some of my happiest hours, I rely on the darkness of the night and the quietness of the evening calm, and the companionship of one of my most cherished friends, my faithful shepherd, Turbo.

I am inspired by people who carry the fire within them throughout their lives. Musician Frankie Valli is one of those people who impresses me thoroughly. I recently saw him perform, and he completely had the crowd's rapt attention. He's been performing since he was a teenager, and now, at 74 years old, he gave us an incredible performance. It is a wonderful time we live in when people like Valli are dedicating themselves to their craft.

In addition to loving music and concerts, I love to travel. The Monterey Peninsula in California is one of my favorite places. I think it is the most beautiful area I have ever visited anywhere in the world. I have been going to Pebble Beach in August for the last decade to escape the high humidity in Atlanta. The golf courses in Pebble Beach are the very best anywhere. Jack Nicklaus once said that if he had one last round of golf to play, he would play it at Pebble Beach.

I also love visiting St. Barts and Martha's Vineyard. Traveling is a wonderful way to relax and enjoy what this beautiful country has to offer. But it's not long before I'm ready to get back to work!

I am a huge golf enthusiast and I love to watch the game as well as play it. By far and away, the most exciting time of the golf year is the Masters. Just saying the word sends chills down my spine. It is played every year at Augusta National in Augusta, Georgia—hallowed ground, in my opinion. The legendary Bobby Jones has his fingerprints all over it.

I have been very fortunate to have played Augusta National many times in my life. My fondest memory takes me back to January 1976.

I had been invited to play by my friend, Phinizy Timmerman, chairman of the Graniteville Mills in South Carolina and an Augusta member. He was competitive as all get-out, and he always wanted to beat me in the worst way.

On this particular day, we played 36 holes of golf. On the 33rd hole of the day, the 15th hole, a very difficult par-5, I hit my third shot in the water and Phinizy parred the hole. With his par and my double bogey, we were dead even for the day.

We approached the famous par-3 16th hole deadlocked, and Phinizy was itching to beat me. We each hit seven irons off the tee, and his ball landed about 2 feet from the hole. It looked like he was going to take the lead with a short birdie putt. Then I teed off, and the ball landed just beyond the hole and spun back in the cup for a hole in one.

There is a famous pond near the side of the hole, and I know I could have literally walked across the water to the green to watch Phinizy's putt; I was in a daze. I had just made a hole in one at Augusta! How could I have possibly gotten my feet wet?

There is so much history on that famous hole. When Tiger Woods chipped in from above the green a few years back, it further cemented the great history of the Masters, Augusta National, and the par-3 16th. Jack Nicklaus made a great birdie on that hole to win the Masters at age 46. And I made a hole in one there to beat my friend Phinizy.

When Tiger Woods chipped in on the 16th hole at Augusta, basically icing another Masters win, do you think he was riding on emotion? Did you see his face, the fist pump, and the adrenaline flowing? No one can tell me that emotion and passion didn't have a lot to do with his success. The same is true of the 2008 Ryder Cup team. People have wondered why the American team seems to always have trouble beating the Europeans, and we finally won one. You can't tell me that didn't have to do with the camaraderie and enthusiasm of those young guys.

And if you want to see some real emotion and passion, come to a University of Georgia football game in Athens. Saturdays at Sanford Stadium are intense. It's hard to describe. The stadium itself seats 94,000 people, and there will be another 20,000 fans outside tailgating. Georgia coach Mark Richt understands the tradition well. He has a special knack for finding ways to get the players on a high, like "Black Out Day," when he asks all the fans to come to the game dressed in black, and the whole stadium turns black for the game.

> *"One of the things I have admired about Fran is that he has always been a great father to his children."*
>
> — PHYLLIS TINGELHOFF

In July 2008, I saw one of the most competitive emotional events of my lifetime. It was the greatest match in the history of Wimbledon, and Roger Federer and Rafael Nadal played a match that lasted 4 hours and 48 minutes—nearly seven hours, with the three rain delays. It was the longest singles final in Wimbledon history, played by two men of extraordinary talent and guts. The passion exhibited by the two of them is hard to fathom. It was a once-in-a-lifetime experience that I'll always remember.

Many people and experts said that Federer was unbeatable. Others said that Nadal was just a clay court champion, that he couldn't play the fast surfaces of Wimbledon. On that day, both played their hearts out. They gave everything of themselves out there on that court.

Why didn't they give up? Nadal won the first two sets, had the match point in hand, and blew match point after match point after match point. What was there inside him to go out and play a fifth set after he came so close to winning so many times, but could not find a way to close Federer out?

And what about Federer? He lost two straight sets and went on to tiebreakers in sets three four, and as if by miracle, he found a way to win the matches. But how could he keep it up?

Both men were so gracious, in victory and in defeat. When I think of competition *par excellence*, I think no further than those two guys. We all have a lot to look forward to as we watch those two face each other. They are both such gracious champions and never make excuses about anything. They have total respect for one another.

Where does the desire come from in guys like Federer or Nadal or Woods? It comes from the inside and you either have it or you don't. I had it in every sport I ever played, and I have it in business and in life.

Sam Walton might have been the greatest businessman of all time. The company he built himself from the ground up today earns more revenue than any company in the world. He had a focus on the customer like no one I have ever known. It never was about Mr. Sam; it was always about focusing the business around giving low prices and great value to the customer.

I once asked him if he'd ever made mistakes in his business. "Oh, a lot of mistakes," he said. I asked him for one. He said, "I knew the customer wanted low prices and great value. But I didn't realize they wanted the lowest prices and the greatest value on *branded* products."

So what did he deliver to the customer? The customer saw low prices on the branded products as well. And that accomplishment has driven the most remarkable business story of my lifetime. It wasn't about how much money he could make; it was providing products that had value and benefit to the customer.

Doing things the right way in business has always been very important to me, too. Two of my children work with me now. Can you imagine how I would feel if they weren't proud of how we do business? I am not sure if a businessman can have more important credentials and credibility than when he has his children working with him.

Walton had another ingredient to his businesses that made him successful. He wanted to be sure the customer was treated with the utmost of respect, and he provided the greatest customer service that the retail industry had ever known. I've taken that lesson to heart. It is not about us, it is about customers in the business world and it is about others in our personal life. And if we always keep this in mind, our businesses will prosper and our personal life will always be on a high note.

In business, you have to find a way to adapt to the circumstance you are presented with. I have had the ability to do that through the years. I learned the game of professional football with the new franchise team in Minnesota, and had perhaps my best years in football in New York, with the Giants.

Some of my teammates saw this in me: the ability to perform and take charge of a given situation. This comes from learning and having a confidence level in what you learn.

One of the loves of my life, my shepherd Turbo, has learned to adapt. He can't hear any longer so he adapts and does just fine. I have spent the past 12 years with him. I spend hours at a time with him. All my dogs are human to me. They are caring and they have feelings. They are magnificent, bright, and beautiful, and all they want to do is please me.

My family is, and always was, the most important thing in my life. None of the desire or the fire inside for athletics came from my parents. They would not have known how to give me that. But my parents are the most wonderful human beings, and I learned so much from each of them. I am who I am because of them.

Dad was the most decent human being I have ever known. He had to fight for everything in his life; nothing came easy for him.

There was not a bad bone in his body. He was such a kind soul. My son Matthew, I am proud to say, is a lot like him.

My mom was the competitor—she was the feisty one in the family. She raised three boys and cleaned rooms, which we rented out. She had a wonderful work ethic. She was also very talented. She could play the piano and was a great woman of faith. After Dad died, she became a preacher and did a lot of traveling.

My brother, Dallas, was also a great entrepreneur. I probably spent more time with Dallas than my younger brother, Wendell, because we were closer in age, but I love and respect them both dearly. They both are smart and have done very well in life. They both reside in the Atlanta area and we remain close.

My wife Linda is my life. She is my best friend and closest companion. We do everything together and I am overwhelmed by the love we have for each other. She is the best cook in the history of the world and a wonderful and remarkable woman. She understands me and we have so much enjoyment spending our lives together.

"Fran is absolutely the very best person I have ever known. He is my best friend in the whole world and the pride and joy of my life."

—Linda Tarkenton, wife of Fran Tarkenton

I can't imagine life without my four children. I want them to find everything they want in life, and to be comfortable in their skin. I want them to be kind, have good ethics, good morals, and be happy about who they are. I want them to be happy with themselves.

Mt first born, Angela, is a hard-charger. She has incredible ethics, is very comfortable with herself, and is a great mother of her children. She works with me in my Atlanta office and does a terrific job. Being around her every day is such a joy.

My son Matthew also works with me and, as I mentioned, reminds me so much of my dad. He is a kind soul and is smart and good and so much fun to be around.

Melissa is probably the most competitive of my kids. She has good street smarts. She is a terrific mother to her children and has done a wonderful job raising her family. I am proud of what she has become and cherish the time I spend with her.

My youngest daughter Hayley is in college now, and I really miss her. She is so precocious, and has a heart as pure as a person could have. She loves animals and is extremely talented in so many ways.

I am still amazed that after over 30 years since I retired from playing professional football, I still receive about 20 pieces of correspondence a day from fans—everything from requests for various items, to signing footballs, football cards, pictures, and letters. I am truly humbled by all of it.

I really love life. I live it fully and I do it unabashedly. I love my family, my wife, my children, my grandchildren, my friends, and my dogs. I have a special way of working with everybody. I treat them all with respect and kindness, and I thoroughly enjoy every day.

I have had some fantastic experiences in my life with football and business success, but nothing I have achieved comes close to what my family has meant to me. Without them, none of it would have meant anything. My passions, my loves, and everything I value centers on them. I am so thankful to have them in my life. I could never have asked for more.

CHAPTER 16

The Best of It All

Sports, sports, sports—it was my whole life for so long. My heroes Sammy Baugh and Jack Scarbath inspired me with their play. In Athens, the Whatleys, Billy Henderson, and Weyman Sellers inspired me person-to-person. I don't think they will ever know what they meant to me.

I sometimes wonder what would have happened in my life if things had gone a little differently. What if I had decided to go to Auburn or Georgia Tech? What if Coach Butts had sent Charlie Britt onto that field before I had the chance to call my first play? What if Quentin Lumpkin hadn't gotten to me before I left for Florida State? What if I had walked on the grass at training camp in Mankato?

Amusing as it may be to imagine what might have been, I am a part of all that I have met and all that I have experienced. And I wouldn't have it any other way.

I remember Dallas and those narrow D.C. alleys, our first house in Athens, and the lot between the church and the parsonage where we played. I recall the field nearby where I learned to throw a football and the YMCA where Chester Leathers and I spent so much of our time.

Sports, sports, sports—it was my whole life for so long. My heroes Sammy Baugh and Jack Scarbath inspired me with their play. In Athens, the Whatleys, Billy Henderson, and Weyman Sellers inspired me person-to-person. What special people they were! I don't think they will ever know what they meant to me.

The great competition with Charley Britt and Tommy Lewis for the starting quarterback position in Georgia was defining for me. And I went into the Texas game without being sent in because I had to. I felt the same way when I thought Alex Webster was going to cut Bob Tucker in New York, and when I thought that Mike Lynn was going to release Ahmad Rashad.

All those characters that were brought into training camp those first few years, as the Vikings tried to establish themselves in the National Football League, were such amazing people. It was a long struggle and I was glad to have been a part of it.

I had the opportunity in the early years to make so many great friendships.

There were tests along the way, like my differences with Norm Van Brocklin, but I am grateful for what he taught me during the six years that I was with him in Minnesota.

The trade to the New York Giants was really a great thing for me in my career. I was in my prime in New York, and loved my teammates and the fans. And I really enjoyed playing for Allie Sherman and Alex Webster in New York, and I truly fell in love with the city.

Move over, 80-year-old entrepreneurs—Fran Tarkenton is only a little over a decade away. And the fire is still burning.

There is no place in the entire world like New York City. And when those cab drivers still yell at me after all those years, "Hey Fran," and give that little hip shake? Well, it really means a lot to me.

How lucky I was, after my wonderful years in New York, to return to my professional football roots, when I was traded back to the Minnesota Vikings. It was really special to come home again. I was so fortunate to be back with so many of my original teammates and be a part of some of the greatest teams to ever play in the National Football League. Plus I got to meet Bud Grant and Jerry Burns.

I said before that it was such a privilege to be able to just watch Jim Marshall play the game of football. What a player and what a special person he is. There has never been and will never be anyone like him.

All those Super Bowls and great Viking teams will forever mean so much to me.

When I took the knee in the final game of the 1978 season, the part of my life that lived with me and inside me every minute was over, but the entrepreneurship in me had risen. It is a fire that has stayed with me for many decades, and hopefully for many more to come. Move over 80-year-old entrepreneurs— Fran Tarkenton is only a little over a decade away. And the fire is still burning.

* * *

I was talking to my good friend Roger Staubach about a year ago. For the first time in our very long friendship, we talked about that fateful Hail Mary game. You know the one I mean—when he threw that pass to Drew Pearson and knocked our best-ever Vikings team out of the playoffs.

I told him about watching the game replay at my lake home that previous fall, and how I felt reliving it. He told me about what was going through his mind during that play. He also remembered what had happened on the play before, when a security guard on the sideline kicked Pearson in the leg after he caught the pass that gave the Cowboys a first down around midfield. Cowboys coach Tom Landry's wife also saw the kick and reported it to the league the next day. After reviewing the game films, the league called the Vikings, and noted longtime security employee Dick Jonckowski was banned from the playing field for two years following the incident. Apparently, the guard had kicked at the ground in disgust at the official's call for a complete catch, and the frozen turf compelled his foot into the receiver. Roger, a little tongue in cheek, told me that he purposefully underthrew Pearson so that he could catch the ball on his hip for the winning touchdown.

It was a great conversation, one I had never had before with him about the game. It also brought me back to some other fond memories that we had together.

Years ago, we worked on a commercial together for Carrier Air Conditioning. We had an "argument" in the commercial that defined the product. Roger would say, "It's an air conditioner," and I would shoot back, "It's a heater."

Sometime after we filmed the commercial, the Vikings were hosting a game against the Cowboys. Back in those days, both teams were situated on the same sideline.

During the game there was a first-down measurement taking place by the officials right in front of the Dallas bench, and directly in front of Dallas Coach Tom Landry. I was standing there on the field and Roger was right there on the sideline next to his coach.

I looked over at Roger and said, "It's a heater." And Roger looked at me and said, "It's an air conditioner." And Coach Landry—much too serious for anyone to be—needed a full explanation as to what that was all about.

It saddens me to see the league as it is today. The wealthy owners have so much control over their franchises and take the credit for what is happening in the NFL. In my day, an owner would not think of ever coming into a locker room. Today, the owners think they are representative of the National Football League because they went out and bought a franchise. Well, they are not.

The players are the ones who built the league. The real fabric of the NFL is the great players of the past and the owners who paid their dues, like the Maras in New York, the Rooneys in Pittsburgh, and the Max Winters in Minnesota.

It is in others like Fred Zamberletti, the great trainer of the Vikings, who has been with the organization since its inception, and in the late Stubby Eason. These are the ones who truly represent the National Football League. And they should be getting the credit.

In December 2008, I ventured with a friend to Athens, Georgia, to explore the places I remember from my childhood, which provided the opportunity to revisit the places I so fondly remember.

Although it was many years ago that I lived there, it seemed as if it was yesterday when we pulled into Athens. The first place we stopped at was my old high school, which has since been renamed Clarke Central High School.

The school looked the same to me, though I had not been back for almost 50 years. I stood on the free throw line where Chester Leathers had counted 113 in a row for me, and the football field where coaches Weyman Sellers and Billy Henderson taught me the fundamentals. I looked out on the spot where we ran laps before every practice. And I remembered how those days made practices at Georgia and training camps with the Vikings and Giants easy, as compared to what my high school coaches put me through.

We visited the home that we lived in, which was next to my father's church, and the playground where I played so many games. It was the place where Mae Whatley discovered me and took me under her wing.

Outside of my mother, there was no more important woman in my life growing up than Mae Whatley. She helped me in school and taught me how to learn. She helped me to believe in myself, and convinced me that I was intelligent and had a great future ahead of me.

We visited the site where the Athens YMCA once stood, and I acknowledged my love for Coburn Kelley. We had two hot dogs and a coke at the Varsity Café. From there, we drove over to Sanford Stadium on the University of Georgia campus. On the way, we passed former coach Wally Butts' old house, where he tried to convince me and others to return to the team.

Sanford Stadium was a playground for me and it holds so many memories. In the left corner of the far end zone opposite the street side is where in high school I returned a kickoff 99 yards for a touchdown against Valdosta High School. It is also the same location where I threw a pass to Bill Herron for the winning touchdown in the SEC championship game.

And at midfield is where I threw a lateral to Jack "Buffalo" Smith in the famous game-ending play against Elberton High School. It was an unbelievable play. We were in a classic battle with Elberton "between the hedges" as it was called at Sanford Stadium. We were behind, and it was the last play of the game. We started at our own 40-yard line, and I started running around and was able to work my way to the 50, and there was Jack "Buffalo" Smith running with me.

If we had run into Bud Grant and Norm Van Brocklin having coffee at the outside tables with Allie Sherman and Alex Webster, I think the day would have been complete.

As I was about to be tackled, I threw a lateral pass to him and he went untouched the final 50 yards for a touchdown to win the regional championship for Athens. Jack had never carried the ball before in a game and had never touched the ball on an offensive play. And after his historic run, he was offered a scholarship to play at Clemson.

I visited my dormitory, Payne Hall, where I lived when I went to the University of Georgia. Quentin Lumpkin was with me as I traveled through the Georgia campus. And he is with me everywhere I go.

I visited the Georgia Hall of Fame building, the Georgia Bulldogs' locker room and coaches' area, where the team was preparing for a bowl game. It had changed some, but it still held that special feeling.

I started that day with a visit with Ruth Brooks and ended it with the president of Aviva Life Insurance Company. En route, I found the memories of my roots at my old high school, memories of Weyman Sellers and Billy Henderson, and the free throw line. Our first house in Athens, the field where Mae Whatley and I first met, and Sanford Stadium. We saw the Athens Y where Coburn Kelley impacted my life, Coach Butts' house, and the dormitory where I was saved by Quentin Lumpkin.

After my meeting with the president of Aviva at a small deli in Athens, if we had run into Bud Grant and Norm Van Brocklin having coffee at the outside tables with Allie Sherman and Alex Webster, I think the day would have been complete. Seeing my brother Dallas and his wife Mayree was a wonderful way to end the day. My traveling companion told me that the best part of the visit was the smile on Dallas' face when he recognized me in the driveway of his home.

The experience made me reflect on the whole of my life and the three people who have influenced me more than any others. Coburn Kelley, Quentin Lumpkin, and Bud Grant are larger than life to me.

Kelley taught me ethics and sportsmanship. He taught me about life. He was principled, a terrific leader, and a great role model. He was the closest thing to God on earth to us as kids. We all looked up to him. To us, he was perfect.

Lumpkin was soft-spoken but formidable. The force of his character and his strength and leadership made a huge impression on me.

There is so much I can say about Grant. He was quiet, very measured in his thinking, and always gave the impression that he knew more than you. And the fact is, he did. He never uttered one single word that didn't make sense. He never had a negative thing to say. He had a way of putting everything into the sharpest focus and perspective. He was simple, straightforward, and right to the point. That was Bud, and he was special.

*   *   *

I want to finish here with a wonderful story about an incredible woman by the name of Wilmer Ree Massey, who happens to be the mother of my sister-in-law, Mayree. This story, to me, underscores what life should be about: love.

Wilmer Ree is a wonderful 96-year-old lady. Her son, Dempsey, is 75 years old. He has spasticity, or muscular hypertonicity, which is a disorder of the central nervous system where certain muscles receive a message to tighten and contract. He was not expected to live to the age of 35. The illness has complicated virtually everything he does, and his mother has provided constant care for him for the past 75 years.

Recently, Dempsey became very sick and was hospitalized. It was almost certain he would need long-term hospice care. The doctors told Mrs. Massey that he likely would not be able to go home again because he would need to be in a place that could take care of him and meet all of his needs, likely for the duration of his life.

She politely told the doctor, "Thank you, but we will take Dempsey home in the morning. God has taken care of us and he is going to continue to take care of us."

Then she turned to Dempsey and said, "Your father left us a while back and God has taken care of us, so go to sleep now, and God will make you better."

And the next day he *was* better. The doctor called it a miracle. Wilmer Ree just said, "Every day with Dempsey has been a pleasure for me." And she took him home.

The love between Wilmer Ree Massey and her son, Dempsey, is a special story for me, and I'm very appreciative for the opportunity to be able to share it with you, along with all the other parts of my life.

Thanks for taking the time to come along with me on this wonderful ride. I hope you have enjoyed being with me as much as I have enjoyed being with you.

Afterword

When God made Fran Tarkenton, he broke the mold. Our father is truly one of a kind. As his four children, we have had the unique opportunity to watch, experience, and hear the amazing and varied stories of his life. *Every Day Is Game Day* brings his stories to life. His tremendous accomplishments, rich friendships, and unrivaled generosity of spirit offer inspiration.

Fran Tarkenton—the scrambler, the entrepreneur, the friend, and the father—is as hard to describe as he was to catch on the football field. From his humble beginnings in Richmond, Virginia and Washington, D.C., we witness the bedrock provided by his parents and brothers, of his athletic prowess, business acumen, caring spirit, and dogged determination. As he moved to Athens, Georgia, Dad sought out mentors like Coburn Kelley and Mae Whatley, who recognized and nurtured his God-given talents. He has always recognized and appreciated the importance of partners to help him succeed. Life, for him, is a "team sport."

Playing football games from the alleys of Washington, D.C., to the biggest arenas in the world, he established enduring relationships with everyone from future Hall of Famers to locker room attendants. In a way only he can, Dad tells amazing stories from his sensational moments at Georgia and in the NFL to life lessons, like "seeing the signs" in life. He vividly recalls details from games like the Vikings' heartbreaking loss to the Dallas Cowboys in 1975, the day he not only lost the game, but also his father. In football and in life, one of Dad's most admirable traits is his ability to rise from the ashes of the most challenging moments.

For most professional athletes, "retirement" from playing is the beginning of the end. For Dad, however, every day truly is game day. He is and will always be a player in the game of life. He is always at the center of the action.

Since football, Dad has been more active than ever. He has started multiple businesses in fields as varied as technology, marketing, and insurance. He has built these companies from the dirt. As he did on the field, when he goes one way and finds an obstacle, he changes direction and keeps going until he finds the path to success. Just as Bud Grant quietly showed him how to observe the subtleties of life, Dad finds opportunities where others see dead ends.

He evaluates business partners not by the schools on their resume, their social circles, or the labels on their shirts, but by their face. He is a face reader. He builds relationships with characters that many of us would pass right by. He appreciated and learned from Johnny Carson, Sam Walton, and Hank Aaron—an incredibly wide range of people, and those more unassuming such as Ruth Brooks, Marvin Bluestein, and 97-year-old Pearl in St. Barts. He inspires us all to look for the "character" in each person and to discover the story that each individual has to tell.

Today, as he nears his 70th birthday, our dad has more to teach each of us than ever before. He inspires his family and coworkers as much today as he did his football teammates. He demonstrates an unquenchable passion to accomplish, to improve the lives of others, and to enjoy every moment of the game of life. He gives of his talent and spirit to individuals whenever he can—to people like Brad Carr, who Dad helped reconnect with his family after 50 years!

We are very proud of "Incredible Fran," as our grandmother dubbed him. We hope that each and every one of us can learn from the life he shares in *Every Day Is Game Day*.

Angela
Matthew
Melissa
Hayley

Appendix

Career Statistical Summary

Playing in the National Football League for 18 years is a phenomenal accomplishment in and of itself. Playing at the level that Fran Tarkenton played is nothing short of extraordinary. The following records and statistics enumerate his achievements in professional football over his career of almost two decades, cementing his legacy as one of the greatest quarterbacks of all time.

—Jim Bruton

1961

Fran Tarkenton's first year in professional football started auspiciously. A surprise upset of George Halas' heavily favored Bears was a harbinger of what lay ahead for the rookie from Georgia. Coming off the bench in the first quarter, he led the newly franchised Minnesota Vikings to an astounding 37–13 victory, throwing four touchdown passes and running for another. Although the team would end the season an anemic 3–11, it was the beginning of a successful franchise and a record-setting career.

Passing

Tm	G-GS	Cmp	Att	Yds	TD	Int	Y/A	Y/G	Sk	QBrec
MIN	14-10	157	280	1,997	18	17	7.1	142.6	na	2-8-0

Rushing

Tm	Att	Yds	TD	Lng	Y/A	Y/G	A/G	YScm	RRTD	Fmb
MIN	56	308	5	52	5.5	22	4	308	5	8

1962

By 1962, Tarkenton was starting every game for Norm Van Brocklin's Vikings. He completed 22 touchdown passes on the year, third-most in the league in just his second NFL season, and threw for 2,595 yards. His predilection for scrambling and his uncanny ability to find open receivers while running from one side of the field to another excited crowds like few quarterbacks before or after him.

Passing

Tm	G-GS	Cmp	Att	Yds	TD	Int	Y/A	Y/G	Sk	QBrec
MIN	14-14	163	329	2,595	22	25	7.9	185.4	na	2-11-1

Rushing

Tm	Att	Yds	TD	Lng	Y/A	Y/G	A/G	YScm	RRTD	Fmb
MIN	41	361	2	31	8.8	25.8	2.9	349	2	5

1963

Tarkenton completed 170 passes, the most to this point in his career, for 2,311 yards. More important, he had become the leader of a Vikings team that was solidifying its own identity as a franchise. He also notched his highest completion percentage and lowest interception total to date.

Passing

Tm	G-GS	Cmp	Att	Yds	TD	Int	Y/A	Y/G	Sk	QBrec
MIN	14-13	170	297	2,311	15	15	7.8	165.1	na	4-8-1

Rushing

Tm	Att	Yds	TD	Lng	Y/A	Y/G	A/G	YScm	RRTD	Fmb
MIN	28	162	1	24	5.8	11.6	2	162	1	7

1964

Just three years after its inception, the Vikings had their first winning season as a franchise, finishing 8–5–1. Tarkenton led the way, throwing 22 touchdown passes and completing 171 passes for 2,506 yards. It was Tarkenton's first Pro Bowl nod. He was becoming one of the most exciting and elite quarterbacks in the league and a fan favorite.

Passing

Tm	G-GS	Cmp	Att	Yds	TD	Int	Y/A	Y/G	Sk	QBrec
MIN	14-14	171	306	2,506	22	11	8.2	179	na	8-5-1

Rushing

Tm	Att	Yds	TD	Lng	Y/A	Y/G	A/G	YScm	RRTD	Fmb
MIN	50	330	2	31	6.6	23.6	3.6	330	2	6

1965

It was another Pro Bowl season for Tarkenton, though his Vikings just broke even on the year at 7–7. But the quarterback's numbers only continued to grow. He threw for a personal-best 2,609 yards, good for third-best in the league among all quarterbacks.

Passing

Tm	G-GS	Cmp	Att	Yds	TD	Int	Y/A	Y/G	Sk	QBrec
MIN	14-14	171	329	2,609	19	11	7.9	186.4	na	7-7-0

Rushing

Tm	Att	Yds	TD	Lng	Y/A	Y/G	A/G	YScm	RRTD	Fmb
MIN	56	356	1	36	6.4	25.4	4	356	1	5

1966

The Vikings disappointed with a 4–9–1 slide. It would also precipitate a departure for the quarterback. His personal totals still ranked among the best in the league as he ended his six-year run with the Minnesota Vikings in a blockbuster trade to the New York Giants.

Passing

Tm	G-GS	Cmp	Att	Yds	TD	Int	Y/A	Y/G	Sk	QBrec
MIN	14-12	192	358	2,561	17	16	7.2	182.9	na	4-7-1

Rushing

Tm	Att	Yds	TD	Lng	Y/A	Y/G	A/G	YScm	RRTD	Fmb
MIN	62	376	4	28	6.1	26.9	4.4	376	4	8

1967

Tarkenton's New York debut was good for huge numbers and a third Pro Bowl selection. He finished second in the NFL with 29 touchdowns. Unfortunately, all those touchdowns didn't translate to big wins. Even so, he was quickly becoming the heart of the Giants franchise and was often compared to his conspicuous crosstown rival Joe Namath.

Passing

Tm	G-GS	Cmp	Att	Yds	TD	Int	Y/A	Y/G	Sk	QBrec
NYG	14-14	204	377	3,088	29	19	8.2	220.6	na	7-7-0

Rushing

Tm	Att	Yds	TD	Lng	Y/A	Y/G	A/G	YScm	RRTD	Fmb
NYG	44	306	2	22	7	21.9	3.1	306	2	4

1968

It was another Pro Bowl season for Fran Tarkenton and another mediocre season for the Giants. Tarkenton had settled into his role, but the pressure for a winning season was strong, ultimately resulting in the dismissal of head coach Allie Sherman.

Passing

Tm	G-GS	Cmp	Att	Yds	TD	Int	Y/A	Y/G	Sk	QBrec
NYG	14-14	182	337	2,555	21	12	7.6	182.5	na	7-7-0

Rushing

Tm	Att	Yds	TD	Lng	Y/A	Y/G	A/G	YScm	RRTD	Fmb
NYG	57	301	3	22	5.3	21.5	4.1	301	3	2

1969

The Pro Bowls were coming routinely for Tarkenton. There was no doubt that he was now one of the premier quarterbacks in all of professional football, but the postseason still eluded him.

Passing

Tm	G-GS	Cmp	Att	Yds	TD	Int	Y/A	Y/G	Sk	QBrec
NYG	14-14	220	409	2,918	23	8	7.1	208.4	36	6-8-0

Rushing

Tm	Att	Yds	TD	Lng	Y/A	Y/G	A/G	YScm	RRTD	Fmb
NYG	37	172	0	21	4.6	12.3	2.6	172	0	7

1970

Tarkenton led the Giants to a 9–5 record in 1970 under second-year head coach Alex Webster. The performance netted him yet another Pro Bowl team, as well as a Pro Football Writers selection for 2nd Team All-NFL.

Passing

Tm	G-GS	Cmp	Att	Yds	TD	Int	Y/A	Y/G	Sk	QBrec
NYG	14-14	219	389	2,777	19	12	7.1	198.4	36	9-5-0

Rushing

Tm	Att	Yds	TD	Lng	Y/A	Y/G	A/G	YScm	RRTD	Fmb
NYG	43	236	2	20	5.5	16.9	3.1	236	2	3

1971

In his last season in New York, Tarkenton compiled significant numbers. He was fourth in the league in pass completion percentage and third in total passing yards. His trade back to Minnesota caused shockwaves around the NFL as strong as those that shook the league when he was dealt to New York.

Passing

Tm	G-GS	Cmp	Att	Yds	TD	Int	Y/A	Y/G	Sk	QBrec
NYG	13-13	226	386	2,567	11	21	6.7	197.5	27	4-9-0

Rushing

Tm	Att	Yds	TD	Lng	Y/A	Y/G	A/G	YScm	RRTD	Fmb
NYG	30	111	3	16	3.7	8.5	2.3	111	3	4

1972

Although Minnesota finished 7–7, Tarkenton was in top form in his first year back with the Vikings. It was clear that the signal caller was happy to be back, this time under a new coach and a new offense under head coach Bud Grant. *The Sporting News* selected Tarkenton to the 1st Team All-Conference.

Passing

Tm	G-GS	Cmp	Att	Yds	TD	Int	Y/A	Y/G	Sk	QBrec
MIN	14-14	215	378	2,651	18	13	7	189.4	26	7-7-0

Rushing

Tm	Att	Yds	TD	Lng	Y/A	Y/G	A/G	YScm	RRTD	Fmb
MIN	27	180	0	21	6.7	12.9	1.9	180	0	3

1973

With Tarkenton at the helm, the Vikings started winning—and winning big. The team won 12 games on their way to his first-ever Super Bowl appearance. Though they lost the championship to the Dolphins, the season ushered in what would become an era of greatness for the men in purple.

Passing

Tm	G-GS	Cmp	Att	Yds	TD	Int	Y/A	Y/G	Sk	QBrec
MIN	14-14	169	274	2,113	15	7	7.7	150.9	31	12-2-0

Rushing

Tm	Att	Yds	TD	Lng	Y/A	Y/G	A/G	YScm	RRTD	Fmb
MIN	41	202	1	16	4.9	14.4	2.9	202	1	5

1974

It was another "super" year for the Vikings, who headed to their second-straight Super Bowl appearance. Tarkenton's numbers were top-tier across the board. But the team would fall just short of the world championship, this time to Terry Bradshaw and the Pittsburgh Steelers.

Passing

Tm	G-GS	Cmp	Att	Yds	TD	Int	Y/A	Y/G	Sk	QBrec
MIN	13-13	199	351	2,598	17	12	7.4	199.8	17	9-4-0

Rushing

Tm	Att	Yds	TD	Lng	Y/A	Y/G	A/G	YScm	RRTD	Fmb
MIN	21	120	2	15	5.7	9.2	1.6	120	2	2

1975

It was the team many Minnesota fans—and indeed, Tarkenton himself—have called the "best Vikings team ever." His numbers were huge, and the accolades came fast and furious—MVP awards from (to name a very few) the Associated Press, Pro Football Writers Association, and the NFL itself. But the dream season came to a screeching halt in the opening round of the playoffs when Roger Staubach completed an improbable pass to Cowboys teammate Drew Pearson, a play that would introduce *Hail Mary* into the football lexicon.

Passing

Tm	G-GS	Cmp	Att	Yds	TD	Int	Y/A	Y/G	Sk	QBrec
MIN	14-14	273	425	2,994	25	13	7	213.9	27	12-2-0

Rushing

Tm	Att	Yds	TD	Lng	Y/A	Y/G	A/G	YScm	RRTD	Fmb
MIN	16	108	2	21	6.8	7.7	1.1	108	2	1

1976

Tarkenton was selected to the *Pro Football Weekly* 1st Team-All-Conference and the UPI 1st Team All-Conference, as well as a staggering ninth Pro Bowl selection. More important, he led the team to its third Super Bowl in four years. The story came to an unfortunately familiar end.

Passing

Tm	G-GS	Cmp	Att	Yds	TD	Int	Y/A	Y/G	Sk	QBrec
MIN	13-13	255	412	2961	17	8	7.2	227.8	25	10-2-1

Rushing

Tm	Att	Yds	TD	Lng	Y/A	Y/G	A/G	YScm	RRTD	Fmb
MIN	27	45	1	20	1.7	3.5	2.1	45	1	4

1977

Tarkenton missed a portion of the season because of injury, but despite that he was still ranked 1ˢᵗ in the NFL in pass completion percentage as well as completed passes per game.

Passing

Tm	G-GS	Cmp	Att	Yds	TD	Int	Y/A	Y/G	Sk	QBrec
MIN	9-9	155	258	1,734	9	14	6.7	192.7	22	6-3-0

Rushing

Tm	Att	Yds	TD	Lng	Y/A	Y/G	A/G	YScm	RRTD	Fmb
MIN	15	6	0	8	0.4	0.7	1.7	6	0	3

1978

It was the 18ᵗʰ and final season for Tarkenton. But the quarterback wasn't done yet. For the first time in his career, he finished first in total passing yards, completing for a staggering 3,468 yards and putting an exclamation point on a superlative career.

Passing

Tm	G-GS	Cmp	Att	Yds	TD	Int	Y/A	Y/G	Sk	QBrec
MIN	16-16	345	572	3,468	25	32	6.1	216.8	27	8-7-1

Rushing

Tm	Att	Yds	TD	Lng	Y/A	Y/G	A/G	YScm	RRTD	Fmb
MIN	24	-6	1	15	-0.3	-0.4	1.5	-6	1	7

Career Passing Totals

GS	Cmp	Att	Yds	TD	Int	Y/A	Y/G	Sk	QBrec
246	3,686	6,467	47,003	342	266	7.3	191.1	274	124-109-6

Career Rushing Totals

Att	Yds	TD	Lng	Y/A	Y/G	A/G	YScm	RRTD	Fmb
675	3,674	32	52	5.4	14.9	2.7	3,662	32	84

Fran Tarkenton finished his 18-year NFL career amassing 47,003 yards (over 26 miles) and 3,686 passes, 342 of them for touchdowns. He also ran for 3,674 yards and scored 32 touchdowns.

In his final seven years with the Minnesota Vikings, he led them to six NFC Central Division titles and to three Super Bowl appearances. Hall of Fame Coach Bud Grant has called Tarkenton "The greatest quarterback who's ever played."

When he finished his career, he held virtually all passing records. Overall, he ranks fifth in career passing yards, third in touchdown passes, and will go down in National Football League history as one of the greatest players and most exciting quarterbacks to ever play professional football. He was elected to the Pro Football Hall of Fame in 1986.

Coauthor's Note

I was at the old Metropolitan Stadium in Bloomington, Minnesota in the fall of 1961, when the Minnesota Vikings defeated the Chicago Bears 37–13 in their first game ever as an expansion franchise in the National Football League. The game wasn't supposed to end the way it did, and the final outcome as recorded represents perhaps the greatest upset win in the history of professional football.

I'll never forget that spectacular fall afternoon, when a 21-year-old rookie quarterback from the University of Georgia by the name of Francis Asbury Tarkenton came off the bench in the first quarter and led the upstart Vikings to victory. He did it by providing the prevailing leadership but he also accomplished it in incredible fashion by offering up possibly the greatest and astonishing of feats in NFL history. He threw four touchdown passes in the game, and when he got tired of throwing the ball, he ran one in for a score. At the time, I gave no inspiring thought of someday being presented with the opportunity to be a part of an autobiography on one of the greatest quarterbacks and most interesting personalities to ever play the game.

Working with Fran Tarkenton on his miraculous journey through life has been an unbelievable and incredible experience, difficult at times to fathom. The only legitimate concern in the whole process has been the ongoing fear of missing something notable in his extraordinary and bigger than life presence.

One would have to initially expect that encompassing his marvelous football career path to the Pro Football Hall of Fame in Canton, Ohio, might suffice. But only capturing his storied gridiron achievements and records would provide a grave disservice to the reader and this remarkable human being. His life is so much more than that.

Fran Tarkenton is truly one of the most amazing personalities I have ever known. In addition to his historic football accomplishments, he has had an even more celebrated career as a television personality and serial entrepreneur. During his lifetime, Fran has not only amassed fabulous football memories, but he has also developed and shared thoughtful and inspirational theories, opinions, and beliefs that define his very being, as well as providing valuable assistance to many others along the way.

I am extremely proud to have been afforded the wonderful opportunity to work with Fran on his autobiography, *Every Day Is Game Day*, which has been a fascinating and unbelievable project.

I have found him to be an incredibly kind and genuine person who is extremely generous to others. He is overwhelmingly passionate and fully engaged in everything he does, living every single day to the fullest. He is a great husband, father, and grandfather, and deeply loyal and completely committed to his gallery of friends.

I feel truly blessed to know Fran Tarkenton, and even more so to be able to call him my friend. I honestly don't think he will ever know how special this is to me.

—Jim Bruton, Author